# The Back·to·Basics Cookbook

EDITORIAL
Food Editor Sheryle Eastwood
Assistant Food Editor Rachel Blackmore
Home Economist Anneka Mitchell
Food Consultant Frances Naldrett
Editorial Co-ordinator Margaret Kelly
Subeditor Ella Martin

PHOTOGRAPHY
Andrew Payne

ILLUSTRATIONS
Greg Gaul

STYLING
Carolyn Feinberg

PRODUCTION
Tara Barrett
Chris Hatcher

COVER DESIGN
Frank Pithers

DESIGN AND PRODUCTION MANAGER
Nadia Sbisa

PUBLISHER
Philippa Sandall

BACK TO BASICS
Includes Index
ISBN 1 86343 010 5

Family Circle is a registered trademark
of IPC Magazines Ltd
Published by J.B. Fairfax Press Pty Ltd by
arrangement with IPC Magazines Ltd

Formatted by J.B. Fairfax Press Pty Ltd
Output by Adtype, Sydney
Printed by Toppan Printing Co, Hong Kong

Distributed by J.B. Fairfax Press Ltd
9 Trinity Centre, Park Farm Estate
Wellingborough, Northants
Ph: (0933) 402330 Fax: (0933) 402234

# CONTENTS

## METRIC MEASURES

| | |
|---|---|
| 1.25 mL | 1/4 teaspoon |
| 2.5 mL | 1/2 teaspoon |
| 5 mL | 1 teaspoon |
| 20 mL | 1 tablespoon |
| 60 mL | 1/4 cup |
| 80 mL | 1/3 cup |
| 125 mL | 1/2 cup |
| 250 mL | 1 cup |

## QUICK CONVERTER

| g | oz | mL | fl oz |
|---|---|---|---|
| 15 | 1/2 | 15 | 1/2 |
| 30 | 1 | 30 | 1 |
| 60 | 2 | 60 | 2 |
| 125 | 4 | 125 | 4 |
| 250 | 8 | 250 | 8 |
| 375 | 12 | 375 | 12 |
| 500 | 16 | 500 | 16 |

## MICROWAVE IT

Where microwave instructions occur in this book a microwave oven with a 650 watt output has been used. Wattage on domestic microwave ovens varies between 500 and 700 watts, so it may be necessary to vary the cooking times slightly depending on the wattage of your oven.

## SPECIAL THANKS

The publisher would like to thank the students and teachers of East Sydney Technical College for their assistance with the production of this book and in particular for the recipe development in Christmas Dinner for Ten.

# FOREWORD

You could presume when you see me flourish those pots and pans on stage or on screen that the skill is innate, effortless, automatic – but oh no, dear reader, much needed to be learned, rehearsed, researched, rehearsed and researched. Those early tentative trial and error days witnessed much trial and alas many an error. That's why I'm delighted to be asked to provide a foreword to this book. In the light of my experiences you will find all the information useful.

So much is presumed by your mother (or father), other cooks, teachers and writers. My first major disaster highlights the need for those basic techniques to be clearly understood. When I moved to my first OWN place – a flat which would now be listed as an apartment or a condo – my good mother, a marvellous, generous, constant, country cook, presented me with her aged copy of the CWA Cookbook (*circa 1929*).

The family had always adored the mother's famous steamed puddings so I decided that my first (the inaugural) dinner should parade my inherited skill. The recipe (with suet and fruit) was followed meticulously but the pudding lay there in the bottom of the bowl and died. Those good CWA women presumed I would know to plunge the bowl into water already on the boil. A plaintive call to the mother took ages to diagnose the cause – Mother, too, expected me to know how to cook such a simple dish.

So young cooks (of all ages) welcome to your primary school of the art. Attend each lesson, do your homework, and you may never be tempted to take-away again.

And to add to the pleasure of achieving good results you'll find the time preparing fine food as enjoyable as the wonderful response from those who share your table with you.

The happiest hours of my life are those spent dining and wining, rewriting the history of the world – and graciously accepting the applause for the wonderful food!

Bernard King

# Getting started

You will find the recipes in this book are written in an easy-to-follow style, with most ingredients available at your supermarket.

✧ Before you start cooking, look at the recipe and read through the method. Then, following the ingredients listing, collect and prepare all the foods you will require. Use the easy Check-And-Go boxes which appear beside each ingredient; simply tick the boxes as you get each item out, then you will have all the ingredients to hand when you start cooking. The ingredients are always listed in their order of use.

✧ The next step is to go through the method and get out the equipment that you will need. You should also check the recipe at this stage to see if the oven will be used and, if so, turn it on to preheat.

✧ Being organised and assembling all your ingredients and equipment before you start will save you time in cooking and cleaning up.

❖

## BASIC WHITE SAUCE RECIPE

Makes 250 mL (8 fl oz)

☑ **30 g (1 oz) butter**
☑ **2 tablespoons plain flour**
☑ **$^1/_4$ teaspoon dry mustard**
☑ **250 mL (8 fl oz) milk**

1   Melt butter in a saucepan, stir in flour and mustard. Cook over medium heat for 1 minute.
2   Remove pan from heat and whisk in milk a little at a time until well blended with butter mixture. Cook over medium heat, stirring constantly until sauce boils and thickens.

**Steaming:** Using this cooking method the food is set over boiling water and cooked in the steam given off. Place the food in a metal basket, on a wire rack, or in a steamer in a saucepan, set 1-2.5 cm ($^1/_2$-1 in) above the water. Tightly cover the pan and cook for the required time. Steaming is a popular way of cooking vegetables and fish for the diet conscious. It is one of the best ways to cook food and retain the maximum number of vitamins and minerals.

**Simmering:** This is when liquids are just hot enough for a few bubbles to form slowly and the bubbles burst below the surface. Simmering takes place at a lower temperature than boiling and should not be confused with boiling.

*Remember to collect and measure your ingredients and to get out the equipment you will need before you start cooking*

**Pan cooking:** The food is cooked in a little fat in a frypan. The most commonly used fats are butter, margarine or oil. When pan cooking you need to make sure that the fat is hot enough so that the food cooks without absorbing too much fat, but the fat should not be too hot or the food will burn.

**Boiling:** This is when liquids are hot enough to form bubbles that rise in a steady pattern and break on the surface. The whole mass of liquid starts to move as the bubbling begins.

**Grilling:** Cooking food by direct dry heat. When grilling meat you should place it on a rack in the grill pan, to allow the fat to drip through. Grilling can be used to cook foods such as steaks, chops and sausages, as well as for browning or toasting the top of denser foods.

**Baking:** Cooking food by indirect dry heat. The food can be cooked covered or uncovered, usually in an oven. Cooking meat in this way is called 'roasting'.

# Getting equipped

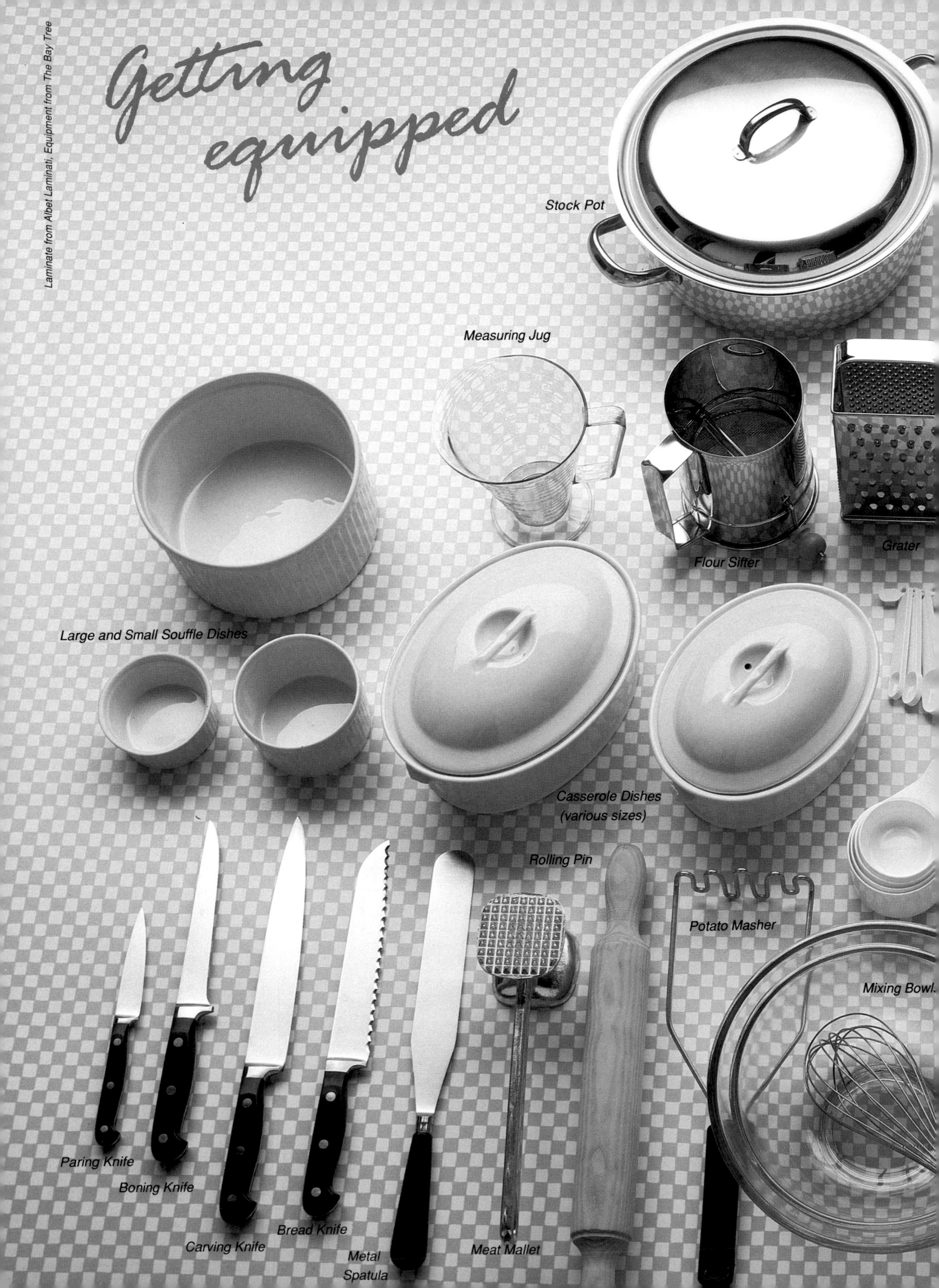

Laminate from Albel Laminati; Equipment from The Bay Tree

Stock Pot

Measuring Jug

Flour Sifter

Grater

Large and Small Souffle Dishes

Casserole Dishes
(various sizes)

Rolling Pin

Potato Masher

Mixing Bowl

Paring Knife

Boning Knife

Carving Knife

Bread Knife

Metal
Spatula

Meat Mallet

Set of Saucepans

Frypan

Colander

Wooden
Spoon

Oven Tray

Tongs

Pastry Brush

Cake Pans

Measuring Spoons

Rubber
Spatula

Measuring Cups

Hand held electric beater

Roasting Pan

BLACK & DECKER
POWER Plus
HEAVY DUTY MIXER

Wire Whisk

Electric Mixer

# Take an egg

'If there's an egg in the house, there's a meal in the house.' When you try these tempting recipes, you will see just how true this is.

❖

## EGGS BENEDICT

*The Hollandaise Sauce used in this recipe is also great served with poached fish, grilled chicken or steamed vegetables.*

Serves 4

- ☐ **2 teaspoons olive oil**
- ☐ **4 spring onions (shallots), sliced**
- ☐ **1 green pepper, thinly sliced**
- ☐ **3 slices ham, chopped**
- ☐ **4 eggs**
- ☐ **2 English muffins, split, toasted and buttered**

HOLLANDAISE SAUCE
- ☐ **3 egg yolks**
- ☐ **3 tablespoons water**
- ☐ **1/4 teaspoon cayenne pepper**
- ☐ **pinch of salt**
- ☐ **180 g (6 oz) butter, clarified**
- ☐ **1 tablespoon lemon juice**

1   Heat oil in a frypan. Cook spring onions and pepper for 3-4 minutes or until tender. Stir in ham and remove from heat.

2   Break eggs into lightly greased poacher cups. Bring 2 cm (³/4 in) of water to the boil, in a frypan large enough to hold the poacher, then lower the heat. Place poacher in pan, cover and simmer for 4-5 minutes or until the whites are firm.

3   To make sauce, place egg yolks, water, cayenne pepper and salt in the top of a double saucepan and whisk until light in colour. Cook over a low heat and whisk constantly until the mixture thickens. Remove from heat and whisk in butter a little at a time. Stir in lemon juice and set aside for 5 minutes to cool slightly.

4   Top muffins with ham mixture, cooked eggs and sauce.

❖

## MUSHROOM SCRAMBLERS

*A more sophisticated version of scrambled eggs, that combines mushrooms, spring onions and fresh sage. If you do not have any fresh sage, try using fresh basil, mint or parsley.*

Serves 4

- ☐ **8 eggs**
- ☐ **2 tablespoons milk**
- ☐ **freshly ground black pepper**
- ☐ **30 g (1 oz) butter**
- ☐ **60 g (2 oz) button mushrooms, thinly sliced**
- ☐ **2 spring onions (shallots), sliced**
- ☐ **2 teaspoons chopped fresh sage**

1   Place eggs and milk in a bowl and, using a whisk, beat to combine. Season to taste with pepper.

2   Melt butter in a medium, heavy-based saucepan. Cook mushrooms, spring onions and sage over a medium heat for 2 minutes. Add egg mixture and cook, stirring gently with a wooden spoon, until egg is set but still creamy. Serve immediately.

---

### RESCUE IT

If Hollandaise Sauce is overheated, or the butter added too quickly, it will curdle. To rescue curdled sauce, whisk together an egg yolk and 1 tablespoon water in a bowl. Transfer hot Hollandaise to a food processor or blender and, with machine running, slowly add egg mixture and process until smooth. Serve immediately.

*Plates from The Bay Tree, Pan from Country Form*

### COOK'S TIP

✧ If scrambled eggs are cooked too quickly, or for too long, liquid is released and they become dark yellow in colour.

✧ For best results, use a wooden spoon and a folding motion when stirring.

✧ Eggs should not be stirred too much during cooking or the texture will be fine and crumbly.

✧ Serve immediately, as scrambled eggs do not reheat successfully.

❖

## SAVOURY SCRAMBLERS

*Scrambled eggs are an all-time favourite breakfast or light meal.*

Serves 4

☐ **8 eggs**
☐ **2 tablespoons milk**
☐ **freshly ground black pepper**
☐ **30 g (1 oz) butter**

1 Place eggs and milk in a bowl and, using a whisk, beat to combine. Season to taste with pepper.

2 Melt butter in a medium, heavy-based saucepan over a gentle heat. Add egg mixture and cook, stirring gently, until the egg mixture is set but still creamy. Serve immediately.

### Variations

**Herb Scramblers:** Stir 1 teaspoon chopped fresh parsley and 1 teaspoon chopped fresh basil into the egg mixture before cooking.

**Curry Scramblers:** Whisk 1 teaspoon of curry powder into the egg mixture before cooking.

### MICROWAVE IT

Prepare mixture as above. Melt butter in a microwave-safe jug or dish and cook on HIGH (100%) for 20 seconds, or until melted. Add egg mixture and cook on HIGH (100%) for 5 minutes, or until egg mixture is set but still creamy. Stir twice during cooking.

*Mushroom Scramblers, Eggs Benedict, Savoury Scramblers*

## ❖
## EGG AND MUSTARD
## HAM ROLLS

*In this recipe the eggs are baked in the oven. These rolls make a great snack or a delicious brunch.*

Serves 4

- ☐ **4 wholemeal rolls**
- ☐ **2 tablespoons wholegrain mustard**
- ☐ **15 g ($^1$/2 oz) butter**
- ☐ **60 g (2 oz) button mushrooms, sliced**
- ☐ **1 onion, chopped**
- ☐ **60 g (2 oz) thin ham slices, cut into strips**
- ☐ **freshly ground black pepper**
- ☐ **4 eggs**
- ☐ **60 g (2 oz) grated cheddar cheese**

1   Cut a slice from the top of each bread roll; set aside and reserve. Scoop out the centre, leaving a thin shell; reserve crumbs for another use. Spread inside of each roll with mustard.

2   Melt butter in a pan and cook mushrooms and onion for 2-3 minutes over a medium heat. Add ham and cook for 2 minutes longer. Divide the mixture between the rolls and sprinkle with pepper.

3   Break an egg into a small bowl, then slide it into a roll. Repeat with remaining eggs and rolls. Sprinkle with cheese and replace the tops.

4   Place rolls on an oven tray and bake at 180°C (350°F/Gas 4) for 25 minutes or until whites are firm.

## Variations

**Egg and Spinach Rolls:** Replace wholegrain mustard with tomato paste, and mushrooms and onion with 6 chopped spinach leaves. Prepare as directed. You may also like to sprinkle the cheese with chopped fresh oregano before baking.

---

### LEFTOVER EGGS

Keep leftover yolks and whites in an airtight container in the refrigerator. Place 1 tablespoon of water over the yolks to prevent a skin forming. Yolks will keep for up to 3 days and whites for up to 10 days. You can freeze whites for up to one month.

---

## Perfect Omelettes

✧   If you do not have a special omelette pan, use an aluminium frypan. Prepare the frypan by rubbing with a small amount of salt and kitchen paper. Remove all traces of salt before cooking. You can also use a nonstick frypan. However if you intend making omelettes on a regular basis it is well worth investing in a good pan.

✧   For best results the butter should be foaming, but not coloured, when you add the egg mixture. This means that the omelette will begin to cook straight away.

## Freshness

The fresher the egg the higher its food value. There are several quick ways to test the freshness of eggs.

✧   When a fresh egg is placed into a glass of water it will sink straight to the bottom.

✧   The yolk of a fresh egg sits in the middle of the egg white when broken onto a saucer.

## FRENCH OMELETTE

*For best results, prepare and cook omelettes quickly and serve immediately. Remember, if the heat is too high, or the omelette is cooked for too long, it will be tough and dry. Try one of these delicious fillings or make your own favourite combinations.*

Serves 1

- ☐ **2 eggs**
- ☐ **1 tablespoon cold water**
- ☐ **freshly ground black pepper**
- ☐ **15 g (¹/2 oz) butter**

1 Lightly whisk together eggs and water; season to taste with pepper.

2 Heat an omelette pan over a medium heat for 1 minute or until hot. Add butter, tipping the pan so the base is completely coated. Heat until the butter is foaming, but not browned, then add the egg mixture. As it sets use a palette knife or fork to gently draw up the edge of the omelette until no liquid remains and the omelette is lightly set.

3 Top with filling of your choice and fold in half. Slip omelette onto a plate and serve immediately.

## AVOCADO AND BACON FILLING

Serves 1

- ☐ **1 tablespoon thick sour cream**
- ☐ **1 teaspoon snipped fresh chives**
- ☐ **¹/2 teaspoon French mustard**
- ☐ **1 tablespoon chopped bacon**
- ☐ **2 tablespoons chopped avocado**

1 Combine sour cream, chives and mustard. Heat a small frypan and cook bacon until crisp. Remove and drain on absorbent kitchen paper.

2 Spread sour cream mixture over one half of omelette, top with bacon and avocado, fold omelette and serve .

*Above left: Egg and Mustard Ham Rolls, Egg and Spinach Rolls*
*Right: Omelette with Vegetarian Filling, Omelette with Avocado and Bacon Filling*

## VEGETARIAN FILLING

Serves 1

- ☐ **1 teaspoon olive oil**
- ☐ **1 tablespoon chopped green pepper**
- ☐ **1 tablespoon finely chopped onion**
- ☐ **¹/2 clove garlic, crushed**
- ☐ **¹/2 tomato, peeled and chopped**
- ☐ **1 black olive, sliced**
- ☐ **1 teaspoon finely chopped fresh basil**
- ☐ **freshly ground black pepper**

Heat oil in a small saucepan. Cook pepper, onion and garlic for 2-3 minutes or until onion softens. Add tomato, olive and basil and cook over a medium heat for 5 minutes longer. Season with pepper.

## *Boiled Eggs*

The way you cook boiled eggs depends on whether you want them soft or hard boiled. Eggs that are at room temperature are less likely to crack during cooking than those taken straight from the refrigerator. The following methods ensure perfect boiled eggs every time.

**Soft boiled:** Bring water to the boil in a saucepan, reduce heat to a simmer and add eggs. Cook for 3 minutes for a light set and 4 ¹/2 minutes for a slightly firmer set.

**Hard boiled:** Place eggs in cold water, bring to the boil, reduce heat and simmer for 10-12 minutes. Remove eggs and place in a bowl of cold water. Peel eggs as soon as they are cool. This prevents the eggs from becoming tough and a dark ring forming around the yolk.

*Pan from The Bay Tree*

# Soups and stocks

The basis of a good soup is a full-bodied stock. It is easy to make stock and well worth the little extra time that it takes. Freeze your homemade stock and use as a quick base for soups, casseroles and sauces.

❖

## FRESH TOMATO SOUP

*Bursting with flavour, this satisfying soup makes a great winter luncheon served with crusty bread, or try it chilled on hot summer days. If you find the soup is too tart, a teaspoon of sugar stirred into it will sweeten the flavour.*

Serves 6

- [ ] **1 tablespoon olive oil**
- [ ] **1 carrot, peeled and chopped**
- [ ] **1 onion, chopped**
- [ ] **2 sticks celery, chopped**
- [ ] **1 clove garlic, crushed**
- [ ] **6 tomatoes, peeled, seeded and chopped**
- [ ] **425 g (14 oz) canned tomatoes, drained and chopped**
- [ ] **1 litre ($1^3/4$ pt) chicken stock**
- [ ] **1 teaspoon chopped fresh thyme, or $^1/4$ teaspoon dried thyme**
- [ ] **$^1/2$ teaspoon Tabasco sauce**
- [ ] **250 mL (8 fl oz) single cream**
- [ ] **2 tablespoons finely chopped fresh basil**
- [ ] **freshly ground black pepper**

1  Heat oil in a large saucepan, add carrot, onion, celery and garlic and cook for 3-4 minutes or until onion softens.

2  Stir in fresh and canned tomatoes, chicken stock, thyme and Tabasco sauce. Bring to the boil and simmer, uncovered, for 30 minutes. Remove from heat.

3  Place in a food processor or blender and process until smooth. Return soup to pan and bring just to a simmer. Remove from heat and stir in cream and basil. Season to taste with pepper.

### HOW MUCH SOUP?

When serving soup as a starter, allow approximately 250 mL (8 fl oz) of soup per person. For soup as a main course, serves may be a little larger.

### CLOUDY CONSOMME?

Consommé should be clear. If your consommé is cloudy it may be because the stock was greasy, unstrained or of poor quality. Whisking the stock after it reaches boiling point or not allowing it to stand before straining will also cause the consommé to become cloudy. Remember that the pan and muslin cloth must be very clean when you are making consommé.

❖

## CONSOMME

*Consommé is the French word for a soup based on meat stock that has been enriched, concentrated and then clarified. It is the simplest, yet most sophisticated, soup and you may serve it hot or cold. The perfect garnish for consommé is thin strips of blanched carrot and leek.*

Serves 6

- [ ] **1 litre (32 fl oz) cold beef stock**
- [ ] **250 g (8 oz) minced beef**
- [ ] **1 small onion, chopped**
- [ ] **1 small carrot, chopped**
- [ ] **1 small leek, chopped**
- [ ] **4 whole peppercorns**
- [ ] **bouquet garni**
- [ ] **2 egg whites, lightly whisked**
- [ ] **1 tablespoon dry sherry**

1  Place stock, beef, onion, carrot, leek, peppercorns, bouquet garni and egg whites in a large saucepan, bring slowly to the boil, whisking continuously. Reduce heat, stir in sherry and simmer gently for $1^1/2$ hours, without stirring.

2  Remove from heat and set aside to stand for 20 minutes. A thick brown scum will have formed on the surface of the stock, skim off and strain carefully through muslin. Remove fat from surface using absorbent kitchen paper.

*Spoon from The Bay Tree*

❖

## CREAM OF MUSHROOM AND HAZELNUT SOUP

*A delightfully creamy soup that makes a great starter for a special occasion. Or, a delicious meal in itself served with crusty French bread and a crispy salad.*

Serves 4

- [ ] **60 g (2 oz) butter**
- [ ] **3 tablespoons flour**
- [ ] **1 litre (32 fl oz) milk**
- [ ] **2 teaspoons oil**
- [ ] **6 spring onions (shallots), chopped**
- [ ] **125 g (4 oz) button mushrooms, sliced**
- [ ] **60 g (2 oz) hazelnuts, toasted, skins removed, and finely chopped**
- [ ] **1 teaspoon paprika**
- [ ] **125 mL (4 fl oz) single cream**
- [ ] **freshly ground black pepper**

1   Melt butter in a medium saucepan. Stir in flour and cook for 1 minute. Remove from heat and gradually stir in milk. Return pan to heat and bring slowly to the boil, stirring constantly. Simmer for 3 minutes, remove from heat and set aside.

2   Heat oil in a medium saucepan and cook spring onions for 2 minutes. Add mushrooms, hazelnuts and paprika and cook for 2-3 minutes longer. Stir in milk mixture, bring to the boil, then reduce heat and simmer gently for 10 minutes.

3   Remove from heat, place in a food processor or blender and process until smooth. Return soup to a clean pan and reheat gently. Stir in cream and season to taste with pepper.

*Consomme, Fresh Tomato Soup, Cream of Mushroom and Hazelnut Soup*

❖

## HEARTY VEGETABLE SOUP

*This soup is very satisfying as a main meal, or you can serve it in smaller quantities as a starter.*

Serves 6

- ☐ **15 g ($^1$/2 oz) butter**
- ☐ **2 teaspoons olive oil**
- ☐ **1 onion, finely chopped**
- ☐ **1 clove garlic, crushed**
- ☐ **4 tomatoes, peeled and chopped**
- ☐ **1 potato, peeled and chopped**
- ☐ **1 cucumber, peeled and chopped**
- ☐ **1.5 litres (2$^1$/2 pt) beef stock**
- ☐ **125 g (4 oz) small shell pasta**
- ☐ **1 tablespoon chopped fresh basil**
- ☐ **1 tablespoon chopped fresh parsley**
- ☐ **1 tablespoon lemon juice**
- ☐ **freshly ground black pepper**

1 Heat butter and oil in a large saucepan and cook onion and garlic for 2-3 minutes or until onion softens. Stir in tomatoes, potato and cucumber and cook for 3-4 minutes longer.

2 Add stock, pasta, basil and parsley. Bring to the boil and simmer for 15-20 minutes or until pasta is tender. Stir in lemon juice and season with pepper.

❖

## MEXICAN CORN CHOWDER

*For a less spicy but just as delicious soup you can omit the chilli.*

Serves 6

- ☐ **15 g ($^1$/2 oz) butter**
- ☐ **2 bacon rashers, rind removed and chopped**
- ☐ **1 onion, finely chopped**
- ☐ **2 sticks celery, chopped**
- ☐ **1 small red chilli, finely chopped**
- ☐ **500 mL (16 fl oz) chicken stock**
- ☐ **1 teaspoon ground cumin**
- ☐ **1 teaspoon dried thyme**
- ☐ **2 tablespoons flour blended with 3 tablespoons milk**
- ☐ **440 mL (14 fl oz) milk**
- ☐ **440 g (14 oz) canned sweet corn kernels, drained**
- ☐ **freshly ground black pepper**

1 Melt butter in a large saucepan and cook bacon, onion, celery and chilli for 4-5 minutes or until onion softens.

2 Add stock, cumin and thyme, bring to the boil and simmer for 10 minutes.

3 Stir in flour mixture, then milk and corn kernels, stir continuously until boiling, then reduce heat and simmer for 3 minutes. Season to taste with pepper.

❖

## PEAR AND TARRAGON SOUP

*You can serve this wonderfully flavoured fruity soup as a starter, or as a dessert soup. To serve as a dessert, stir in 2 tablespoons honey before processing and replace the tarragon with 2 teaspoons ground nutmeg; omit the pepper.*

Serves 6

- ☐ **1 kg (2 lb) pears, peeled, cored and chopped**
- ☐ **250 mL (8 fl oz) water**
- ☐ **185 mL (6 fl oz) white wine**
- ☐ **2 tablespoons lemon juice**
- ☐ **2 tablespoons lime juice**
- ☐ **2 teaspoons chopped fresh tarragon**
- ☐ **freshly ground white pepper**
- ☐ **125 mL (4 fl oz) single cream**

1 Place pears, water, wine, lemon juice, lime juice and tarragon in a large saucepan. Bring to the boil and simmer, uncovered, for 30 minutes.

2 Remove from heat and place in a food processor or blender and process until smooth. Season to taste with pepper and refrigerate until well chilled. Just prior to serving, swirl cream through soup.

❖

## BASIC BEEF STOCK

**Makes 1 litre (1$^3$/4 pt)**

- ☐ **1 kg (2lb) raw beef bones, trimmed of all fat**
- ☐ **2 litres (3$^1$/2 pt) cold water**
- ☐ **6 whole peppercorns**
- ☐ **bouquet garni**
- ☐ **1 onion, chopped**
- ☐ **1 carrot, chopped**
- ☐ **1 leek, chopped**

1 Place bones in a roasting pan and cook, uncovered, at 180°C (350°F/Gas 4) for 30 minutes, or until well browned, turning occasionally.

2 Place bones, water, peppercorns and bouquet garni in a large saucepan. Bring to the boil and simmer gently for 2$^1$/2 hours. Skim occasionally during cooking to remove scum. Add onion, carrot and leek and simmer for a further 1-1$^1$/2 hours. Clarify at end of cooking.

3 Strain stock and cool rapidly.

❖

## VEGETABLE STOCK

Makes 2 litres (3$^1$/2 pt)

- ☐ **2 large onions, quartered**
- ☐ **2 large carrots, roughly chopped**
- ☐ **1 head celery, leaves included, roughly chopped**
- ☐ **1 large bunch parsley, stalks included, roughly chopped**
- ☐ **$^1$/2 teaspoon whole black peppercorns**
- ☐ **2.5 litres (4 pt) cold water**

1 Place onions, carrots, celery, parsley, peppercorns and water in a large saucepan. Bring to the boil, reduce heat and simmer for 30 minutes, stirring from time to time.

2 Remove from heat and allow to cool.

3 Puree cold vegetable mixture, then push through a sieve. Refrigerate or freeze until required.

## Stock making

◇ Use fresh meat and vegetables.

◇ Do not use starchy vegetables, such as potatoes, turnips or parsnips as they will give a cloudy stock. Cauliflower, broccoli or cabbage are too strongly flavoured to be used in stocks.

◇ Stocks based on raw bones have the best flavour and make full-bodied, clear stocks that gel on setting.

◇ Use whole black peppercorns for flavour. Ground pepper turns bitter.

◇ Do not season stock with salt. As stock is an ingredient in other recipes it is better to season the finished dish.

◇ Use cold water for making stock.

◇ Using a deep saucepan will keep evaporation to a minimum.

◇ Long slow simmering makes stock with a full-bodied flavour.

◇ Skim off the scum that rises to the surface during cooking.

◇ Cook fish and seafood stocks for 30 minutes only. A bitter taste can develop if you overcook them.

◇ Skim fat from surface of stock and strain at the end of cooking. Remove fat by dragging strips of absorbent kitchen paper across the surface, or by chilling the stock until the fat solidifies – it can then be lifted off and discarded.

◇ Cool stock before covering. To cool rapidly, place the stock in a pan of ice cubes and stir.

## Storing stock

◇ You can keep stock in the refrigerator for 3-4 days or in the freezer for up to 12 months.

◇ Even if you are only planning to keep it for a few days, stock keeps better in the freezer.

## Clarifying stock

◇ To clarify stock, add an egg shell or lightly whisked egg white to the stock and simmer for 10 minutes. The scum will be drawn to the surface by the egg shell or white and you can then easily remove it. Strain the stock through a fine sieve lined with several layers of muslin.

◇ Before using muslin, it should first be scalded by pouring boiling water over and through it.

*Pear and Tarragon Soup, Hearty Vegetable Soup, Mexican Corn Chowder*

Ladle from The Bay Tree

# Take some mince

Minced meat provides value-for-money meals. A little goes a long way and can be stretched even further by adding soft breadcrumbs or vegetables. It can be made into balls, patties, burgers and loaves.

### SHAPING MINCE
When shaping minced meat, dampen your hands and work on a lightly floured or dampened surface – this will prevent the mince from sticking to your hands and the surface. You will usually need to add an egg to the mince mixture to bind it and make it easier to shape.

## BASIC MEATLOAF

*Serve this meatloaf hot with vegetables as a main meal, or cold cut into slices for sandwiches. Try one of the tasty toppings below to change the flavour completely.*

Serves 4

- [ ] **500 g (1 lb) lean minced beef**
- [ ] **60 g (2 oz) fresh breadcrumbs**
- [ ] **3 tablespoons beef stock**
- [ ] **1 onion, grated**
- [ ] **1 carrot, grated**
- [ ] **2 eggs, lightly beaten**
- [ ] **1 teaspoon dried mixed herbs**
- [ ] **1 teaspoon Worcestershire sauce**
- [ ] **freshly ground black pepper**

1 Place meat, breadcrumbs, stock, onion, carrot, eggs, mixed herbs and sauce in a bowl. Season to taste with pepper and mix well to combine.
2 Press mixture into a lightly greased 20 x 13 cm (8 x 5 in) ovenproof loaf tin and bake at 180°C (350°F/Gas 4) for 40-45 minutes. Drain off liquid, cover and stand for 10 minutes before turning out.

## TEX-MEX TOPPING

- [ ] **125 mL (4 fl oz) tomato sauce**
- [ ] **1 tablespoon barbecue sauce**
- [ ] **1 teaspoon brown sugar**
- [ ] **1 teaspoon chilli sauce**
- [ ] **2 tablespoons finely chopped green pepper**
- [ ] **30g (1 oz) corn chips, crushed**
- [ ] **60 g (2 oz) grated tasty cheese**

Combine tomato sauce, barbecue sauce, brown sugar, chilli sauce and pepper. Turn meatloaf onto an ovenproof plate. Spread Tex-Mex Topping over surface of meatloaf. Top with corn chips and cheese and bake at 200°C (400°F/Gas 6) for 10 minutes or until cheese melts.

## HONEY-GLAZED TOPPING

- [ ] **30 g (1 oz) Mexican pumpkin seeds**
- [ ] **30 g (1 oz) sunflower seeds**
- [ ] **2 tablespoons pine nuts**
- [ ] **2 tablespoons honey**
- [ ] **1 tablespoon brown sugar**
- [ ] **2 tablespoons lemon juice**
- [ ] **$^1/_2$ teaspoon dry mustard**

1 Combine pumpkin seeds, sunflower seeds and pine nuts. Turn meatloaf onto an ovenproof plate and spread top with seed mixture.
2 Place honey, brown sugar, lemon juice and mustard in a saucepan and heat until honey melts and ingredients are blended. Pour mixture over meatloaf and bake at 200°C (400°F/Gas 4) for 10 minutes.

## INDIVIDUAL PASTRY-WRAPPED MEATLOAVES

Serves 4

- [ ] **1 quantity basic meatloaf mixture**
- [ ] **375 g (12 oz) prepared puff pastry, thawed**
- [ ] **1 egg, lightly beaten**

1 Make up basic meatloaf mixture and divide into four equal portions. Divide pastry into four portions. Roll each portion out to a 25 x 12 cm (10 x 5 in) rectangle. Press one portion of meat mixture down the centre of each pastry rectangle.
2 Brush edges of pastry with egg and wrap up like a parcel. Decorate top with leaves cut from pastry scraps. Place rolls on a greased roasting rack in a baking dish. Brush pastry with egg and bake at 180°C (350°F/Gas 4) for 25-30 minutes, or until pastry is golden and crisp.

*Basic Meatloaf with Tex-Mex Topping, Individual Pastry-Wrapped Meatloaves, Chilli Con Carne, Melting Meatballs*

Spoon from Bibelot

## MELTING MEATBALLS

Serves 4

- ☐ **1 quantity basic meatloaf mixture**
- ☐ **90 g (3 oz) tasty cheese, cut into 12 x 1 cm ($^1$/$_2$ in) cubes**
- ☐ **45 g (1$^1$/$_2$ oz) unprocessed bran**
- ☐ **3 tablespoons finely chopped pistachio nuts**
- ☐ **plain flour**
- ☐ **1 egg, lightly beaten**
- ☐ **oil for cooking**

1　Divide meatloaf mixture into twelve equal portions. Wrap one portion of meat around each cheese cube, to make a ball. Repeat with remaining meat and cheese.

2　Combine bran and pistachio nuts. Coat meatballs in flour, dip in egg and roll in bran mixture.

3　Heat oil in a frypan and cook meatballs for 6-8 minutes or until golden brown and cooked through.

## CHILLI CON CARNE

Serves 4

- ☐ **1 tablespoon polyunsaturated oil**
- ☐ **1 onion, chopped**
- ☐ **2 cloves garlic, crushed**
- ☐ **3 small red chillies, finely chopped**
- ☐ **500 g (1 lb) lean minced beef**
- ☐ **$^1$/$_4$ teaspoon ground cloves**
- ☐ **$^1$/$_2$ teaspoon ground cumin**
- ☐ **1 teaspoon dried oregano leaves**
- ☐ **2 teaspoons paprika**
- ☐ **425 g (14 oz) canned tomatoes, undrained and mashed**
- ☐ **1 tablespoon tomato paste**
- ☐ **125 mL (4 fl oz) beef stock**
- ☐ **310 g (10 oz) canned red kidney beans, drained and rinsed**
- ☐ **freshly ground black pepper**

1　Heat oil in a frypan, cook onion, garlic and chilli for 2-3 minutes or until onion softens.

2　Stir in minced beef, cloves, cumin, oregano and paprika. Cook for 5-6 minutes or until meat browns. Combine tomatoes, tomato paste, and stock and pour into pan. Reduce heat and simmer for 20 minutes or until liquid reduces by half.

3　Add kidney beans and cook for 10 minutes longer, or until heated through. Season to taste with pepper.

# Take a piece of steak

Steak is wonderfully versatile. Don't waste the more expensive cuts in the long cooking processes such as stewing; they will lose juices and become tough.

## ❖ BEEF WITH PAPRIKA AND WINE RAGOUT

Serves 4

- ☐ **2 tablespoons olive oil**
- ☐ **750 g (1¹/₂ lb) chuck steak, cut into 2.5 cm (1 in) cubes**
- ☐ **2 large onions, chopped**
- ☐ **2 cloves garlic, crushed**
- ☐ **15 g (¹/₂ oz) butter**
- ☐ **1 tablespoon plain flour**
- ☐ **2 tablespoons paprika**
- ☐ **425 g (14 oz) canned tomatoes, undrained and mashed**
- ☐ **125 mL (4 fl oz) red wine**
- ☐ **125 mL (4 fl oz) beef stock**
- ☐ **freshly ground black pepper**
- ☐ **125 g (4 oz) thick sour cream or unflavoured yogurt (optional)**

1   Heat oil in a large saucepan, cook meat cubes a few at a time, until colour changes. Remove from pan and set aside. Continue browning remaining meat.

2   Add onions to the pan and cook for 4-5 minutes or until golden. Stir in garlic and cook for 1 minute longer. Remove from pan and set aside.

3   Melt butter in the same pan, blend in flour and paprika and cook over a medium heat for 1 minute. Combine tomatoes, wine and stock. Pour into pan. Cook over a medium heat until mixture boils and thickens. Reduce heat. Return meat and onion mixture to the pan. Season to taste with pepper. Cover and simmer for 2 hours, stirring occasionally.

4   Remove pan from heat just prior to serving. Stir in sour cream to give a creamed, marbled effect.

### Variation

**Easy Beef Curry:** Omit paprika and replace with curry powder. Omit wine and during the last 30 minutes of cooking add 3 tablespoons chopped dried apricots, 1 tablespoon sultanas and 1 tablespoon fruit chutney. Replace the sour cream with coconut milk.

## ❖ BEEF WITH SWEET AND SOUR SAUCE

Serves 4

- ☐ **2 tablespoons oil**
- ☐ **500 g (1 lb) lean rump steak, cut into thin strips**
- ☐ **1 onion, cut into eighths**
- ☐ **2 cloves garlic, crushed**
- ☐ **1 teaspoon grated fresh root ginger**
- ☐ **100 g (3¹/₂ oz) oyster mushrooms, sliced**
- ☐ **2 sticks celery, sliced diagonally**
- ☐ **2 carrots, sliced diagonally**
- ☐ **¹/₂ red pepper, chopped**
- ☐ **¹/₂ green pepper, chopped**
- ☐ **425 g (14 oz) canned baby corn, drained**
- ☐ **100 g (3¹/₂ oz) mange tout (snow peas), trimmed**

SAUCE
- ☐ **2 teaspoons chilli sauce**
- ☐ **2 tablespoons white vinegar**
- ☐ **2 tablespoons tomato sauce**
- ☐ **2 tablespoons brown sugar**
- ☐ **2 tablespoons dry sherry**
- ☐ **1 tablespoon cornflour, blended with 125 mL (4 fl oz) pineapple juice**

1   Heat oil in a frypan or wok. Stir-fry meat for 2-3 minutes or until it changes colour. Remove meat and set aside.

2   Add onion, garlic and ginger to the pan and stir-fry for 1 minute. Stir in mushrooms, celery, carrots, red and green peppers, corn and mange tout. Stir-fry for 2-3 minutes. Remove from pan and set aside.

3   To make sauce, combine chilli sauce, vinegar, tomato sauce, brown sugar, sherry and cornflour mixture. Pour into pan and cook for 1 minute or until mixture boils and thickens. Return meat and vegetables to the pan. Stir-fry for 1-2 minutes longer.

## BEEF WITH SATAY SAUCE

Serves 6

☐ **750 g (1¹/₂ lb) lean topside or boneless blade steak**

MARINADE
☐ **2 tablespoons light soy sauce**
☐ **2 teaspoons cornflour**
☐ **2 tablespoons honey**
☐ **1 teaspoon grated fresh root ginger**
☐ **1 clove garlic, crushed**
☐ **1 teaspoon grated lemon peel**
☐ **1 tablespoon dry sherry**

SATAY SAUCE
☐ **125 g (4 oz) peanut butter**
☐ **3 tablespoons finely chopped, unsalted peanuts**
☐ **185 mL (6 fl oz) chicken stock**
☐ **4 tablespoons dry white wine**
☐ **1 tablespoon soy sauce**
☐ **1 teaspoon grated lemon peel**
☐ **1 teaspoon grated fresh root ginger**
☐ **1 clove garlic, crushed**
☐ **1 teaspoon chilli sauce**
☐ **¹/₂ teaspoon curry paste (vindaloo)**

1   Trim meat of all visible fat, cut into 2.5 cm (1 in) cubes and thread onto twelve oiled bamboo skewers.
2   To make marinade, combine soy sauce, cornflour, honey, ginger, garlic, lemon peel and sherry in a glass bowl. Add meat and set aside to marinate.
3   To make sauce, place peanut butter, peanuts, stock, wine, soy sauce, lemon peel, ginger, garlic, chilli sauce and curry paste in a saucepan. Cook over a low heat for 2-3 minutes or until heated through and all ingredients are well blended.
4   Remove satays from marinade and grill for 5-6 minutes, turning and basting with marinade frequently during cooking. Serve with satay sauce.

---

### THE PERFECT STEAK

Everyone has their own preference on how they like their steak cooked; steak can be cooked to rare, medium-rare and well-done. Rare meat is springy to touch, medium meat less springy and well-done has very little give in it. When testing, press with blunt tongs. Do not pierce or cut the meat with a knife as this causes loss of juices and dryness.

---

## STEAK WITH A DEVILLED MARINADE

Serves 4

☐ **4 boneless rib-eye steaks (scotch fillet)**

MARINADE
☐ **1 teaspoon curry powder**
☐ **2 tablespoons brown sugar**
☐ **2 tablespoons tomato sauce**
☐ **2 teaspoons Worcestershire sauce**
☐ **1 teaspoon soy sauce**
☐ **2 teaspoons lime juice**

1   Trim meat of all visible fat and set aside.
2   To make marinade, combine curry powder, sugar, tomato sauce, Worcestershire sauce, soy sauce and lime juice in a glass bowl. Add meat and set aside to marinate for 2-4 hours.
3   Remove meat from marinade, grill on medium-high heat for 3-4 minutes each side. Baste frequently with marinade during cooking.

---

*Meaty Matters*

**Marinating:** This is a clever way of tenderising and adding flavour to less tender cuts of meat. To make a basic marinade you require oil; flavourings, such as herbs and spices; and an acid ingredient, such as wine, soy sauce, lemon juice or a wine vinegar, to break down tough meat fibres. Place the meat and marinade in a bowl, cover and store in the refrigerator until required. The quantity of marinade should be just sufficient to form a pool to coat the meat. Turn the meat occasionally during marinating to ensure all sides come in contact with the marinade.

**Stir-frying:** This is a very quick method of cooking. The meat is usually cut into strips, across the grain, to ensure quick even cooking. For best results, cook meat in batches of no more than 500 g (1 lb). Use a medium-high heat and move the meat back and forth in the pan constantly for 2-3 minutes or until it just changes colour. The addition of vegetables adds flavour, texture and nutrients, making this type of meal one that all the family will look forward to.

---

### MEAT TENDERNESS

Use only the less tender cuts of meat, such as chuck, skirt, blade or round, for making ragouts. These cuts are from the more active part of the animal, so are made up of more fibres and connective tissue, therefore require slow, moist cooking for tenderness.

---

*From left: Steak with a Devilled Marinade, Beef with Paprika and Wine Ragout, Beef with Satay Sauce, Beef with Sweet and Sour Sauce*

# Dinner for two

This menu will serve two people. For four serves, the meat quantity will remain the same, but you will need to double the quantities of the vegetable dishes.

## Setting a table

The most exciting part of having a dinner party is creating an atmosphere. The table can be compared to a stage, where the food and setting inspire the mood for the occasion. The setting can also allow your personal artistic ability to flourish. The choice of dinner ware and cutlery will depend on your menu, however there are a few logical rules you should remember.

*Glasses from Villeroy and Boch*

✧ When you are laying out the cutlery it is usual to place forks to the left of the setting with spoons and knives to the right; the cutting edge of the knives should face inwards. You should arrange the cutlery in the order in which it is to be used, working from the outside, in towards the dinner ware. It is acceptable, and often easier, to have no more than three pieces of cutlery at either side and to place dessertspoons and forks on the table after the main course.

✧ Arrange glasses at the top right-hand corner of each place setting, in the opposite order of use to the cutlery. Working from the inside out, start with the sherry glasses through to champagne flutes.

✧ Colour where possible should co-ordinate; the food, china and table coverings. Your food should be fresh and bright, attractively and simply arranged, giving thought to texture, taste and colour.

❖

## GARLIC POTATO AND CARROT CAKES

Serves 2

- ☐ **1 large potato**
- ☐ **1 small carrot, grated**
- ☐ **1 egg, lightly beaten**
- ☐ **30 g (1 oz) butter**
- ☐ **1 clove garlic, crushed**

1  Boil, steam or microwave potato until partially cooked. Drain and refresh under cold running water. Peel and grate coarsely into a bowl. Add carrot and egg and toss lightly. Season to taste.
2  Divide mixture into four equal portions, shape into rounds and flatten slightly. Melt butter in a frypan and cook garlic for 1 minute. Add potato cakes and cook until golden brown.

❖

## HONEYED SWEET POTATO AND BEETROOT

Serves 2

- ☐ **1 large raw beetroot, peeled and cut into 1 cm (¹/₂ in) width strips**
- ☐ **1 small sweet potato, peeled and cut into 1 cm (¹/₂ in) width strips**
- ☐ **30 g (1 oz) butter**
- ☐ **1 teaspoon grated orange peel**
- ☐ **2 tablespoons orange juice**
- ☐ **2 teaspoons Grand Marnier**
- ☐ **1 tablespoon honey**

1  Boil, steam or microwave beetroot and sweet potato separately until just tender. Drain and refresh under cold running water. Set aside
2  Melt butter in a frypan, stir in orange peel, orange juice, Grand Marnier and honey. Cook over medium heat until honey melts and all ingredients are well blended.
3  Toss in beetroot and sweet potato and cook until heated through. Serve immediately.

### LEFTOVER ROASTS
Cut any leftover beef into slices, place on a plate, spoon over your favourite sauce, cover and reheat in the microwave on MEDIUM (50%) for 3-4 minutes or until heated through. Or fill pitta bread with cold, slices of beef tossed with your favourite salad ingredients. Mince leftovers in the food processor and add to some cooked onions, with flavourings of your choice. Thicken and spoon into an ovenproof dish. Top with a layer of mashed potato and a sprinkling of grated tasty cheese. Bake at 200°C (400°F/Gas 6) for 15-20 minutes or until golden.

❖

## ROASTED BEEF WITH HORSERADISH SAUCE

Serves 2

- ☐ **500 g (1 lb) beef fillet**
- ☐ **freshly ground black pepper**
- ☐ **30 g (1 oz) butter**
- ☐ **3 tablespoons brandy**

HORSERADISH SAUCE
- ☐ **125 mL (4 fl oz) mayonnaise**
- ☐ **125 mL (4 fl oz) unflavoured yogurt**
- ☐ **1 teaspoon lemon juice**
- ☐ **1 teaspoon horseradish relish**
- ☐ **1 avocado, peeled, stoned and chopped**

1  Trim all visible fat from meat and sprinkle with pepper. Tie with string at even intervals to retain the shape during cooking. Heat butter over medium-high heat in a baking dish and sear meat on all sides until golden brown. Spoon brandy over meat and bake at 180°C (350°F/Gas 4) for 20-25 minutes or until cooked as desired, basting frequently with pan juices.
2  To make sauce combine mayonnaise, yogurt, lemon juice, horseradish and avocado in a food processor or blender. Process until smooth. Slice beef and serve with sauce.

*Left: Setting a table*
*Right: Roasted Beef with Horseradish Sauce, Honeyed Sweet Potato and Beetroot, Garlic Potato and Carrot Cakes*

**MENU IDEA**
Serve this main course accompanied by half the quantity of Pear and Tarragon Soup (page 14) as a first course and follow the main course with half the quantity of Nut Bavarian Cream (page 69).

# Roasting

Roasting was originally done over an open fire where very large pieces of meat were turned over glowing embers until cooked through.

## STEP–BY–STEP ROASTING

1  Preheat oven to 180°C (350°F/Gas 4).
2  Trim excess fat and weigh meat to calculate cooking time.
3  Refer to Quick Roasting Guide below for cooking times.
4  After the cooking time is completed, remove meat from the oven and cover with aluminium foil and set aside to stand for 10-15 minutes. This allows juices to settle and makes carving easier.

### Roasting Notes

**Lamb:** Irrespective of the weight, lamb rib loin, rack or crown roast is cooked for 40-55 minutes at 200°C (400°F/Gas 6).
**Pork:** Pork is always cooked to well done as in the Quick Roasting Guide. For puffed, crisp crackling the first 20 minutes of cooking is at 260°C (500°F/Gas 10).

### Keeping it hot

One of the most daunting tasks when serving a hot meal is actually managing to get it to the table hot. If you follow these easy tips your meals will be hot every time.
✧  Start by heating the plates.
✧  You can heat plates by placing them in a warm oven for 10-15 minutes; some ovens contain warming drawers in which plates can be heated.
✧  Plates can also be heated by placing in a sink of very hot water for a few minutes. You need to dry them thoroughly before using.
✧  Have all the food ready before you start serving.
✧  You will find that some foods retain their heat longer than others; for example, whole or large portions of vegetables stay hot longer than slices of meat and smaller cut vegetables, so serve these first.
✧  If your oven size permits, the plates with food on can be returned to the oven, set at 180°C (350°F/Gas 4) and kept warm for up to 10 minutes. Be careful not to overheat as this causes the food to lose moisture and to look unappetising.
✧  Sauces or gravy are best placed in a sauce jug and each person allowed to serve themselves.

## ROASTING IT

There are several methods of roasting. The method you choose will depend on the cut of meat you wish to roast.

**Dry heat roasting:** The meat is first seared to seal in the juices and moisture, then oven-baked at a high temperature for a short period. This way of roasting is ideal for those who enjoy meat browned on the outside and rare in the centre. The more tender cuts of meat, such as beef fillets, boneless sirloin, rump, boneless rib and veal loin should be used for this method.
**French roasting:** The meat is cooked over a bed of chopped vegetables with stock or wine and covered for most of the cooking. The cover is removed towards the end of cooking to brown the meat. Rib roasts, topside, rolled briskets and fresh silverside are the most suitable cuts for this method.
**Pot roasting:** The more economical cuts of meat that would be tough if dry roasted are used for this method. The meat is first seared over a medium-high heat to seal in the juices, then transferred to a covered roasting dish (Dutch oven) and cooked slowly in the oven, or simmered in a covered, large, deep heavy-based saucepan on top of the stove. In both cases the lid must fit tightly. A small quantity of liquid and vegetables can be added if desired and basting is not required. Suitable cuts to use are topside, rolled brisket, thick flank, blade-bone and chuck.

## ROASTING CUTS

Suitable cuts for roasting are –
**Beef:** Blade, Fillet, Rump, Rib Roast, Sirloin, Fresh Silverside, Topside
**Veal:** Leg, Loin, Rack, Shoulder
**Lamb:** Chump, Shoulder, Leg, Mid Loin, Rib Loin, Rack, Crown Roast
**Pork:** Leg, Loin, Shoulder, Foreloin

## QUICK ROASTING GUIDE

|  | COOKING TIME (per 500 g/1 lb) | INTERNAL TEMPERATURE |
|---|---|---|
| RARE | 20-25 minutes | 60°C (140°F) |
| MEDIUM | 25-30 minutes | 70°C (160°F) |
| WELL DONE | 30-35 minutes | 75°C (170°F) |

# Veal

Veal is a very lean, tender, fine-grained meat that cooks quickly. Take care not to overcook veal or it will become tough and dry.

❖

## VEAL CASSEROLE WITH A CHEESY COBBLER TOPPING

Serves 4

- ☐ **4 medium veal steaks, cut into 5 cm (2 in) pieces**
- ☐ **plain flour**
- ☐ **2 tablespoons olive oil**

SAUCE
- ☐ **125 g (4 oz) mushrooms, sliced**
- ☐ **1 clove garlic, crushed**
- ☐ **3 spring onions (shallots), chopped**
- ☐ **1 teaspoon French mustard**
- ☐ **315 mL (10 fl oz) chicken stock**
- ☐ **freshly ground black pepper**
- ☐ **2 teaspoons cornflour blended with 125 mL (4 fl oz) single cream or evaporated skim milk**

CHEESY COBBLER TOPPING
- ☐ **250 g (8 oz) self-raising flour**
- ☐ **pinch cayenne pepper**
- ☐ **pinch chilli powder**
- ☐ **125 g (4 oz) butter**
- ☐ **1 egg, lightly beaten**
- ☐ **125 mL (4 fl oz) milk**
- ☐ **90 g (3 oz) grated tasty cheese**
- ☐ **¹/₂ teaspoon dry mustard**

1  Trim meat of all visible fat and toss in flour. Heat oil in a frypan and cook meat until brown. Transfer to a shallow ovenproof casserole dish.

2  To make sauce, add mushrooms, garlic and shallots to the pan. Cook until mushrooms are soft and place on top of meat. Combine mustard and stock, pour into the pan and bring to the boil, season to taste with pepper. Whisk in cornflour mixture and cook over a medium heat, stirring, until sauce boils and thickens. Spoon over meat and vegetables. Cover and bake at 180°C (350°F/Gas 4) for 40 minutes.

*Left: Glazed Minted Lamb Racks with Roast Vegetables (page 26)*
*Right: Veal Casserole with a Cheesy Cobbler Topping*

3  To make topping, sift flour, cayenne and chilli powder into a large mixing bowl. Rub through 90 g (3 oz) butter until mixture resembles fine breadcrumbs. Combine egg and milk and pour into flour mixture all at once. Stir ingredients together to give a soft, sticky dough. Turn mixture out onto a floured surface and knead lightly. Roll out dough to 1 cm (¹/₂ in) thickness and cut into rounds with a 5 cm (2 in) cutter.

4  Remove casserole dish from oven, uncover and, working quickly, top with scone rounds. Melt remaining butter and combine with cheese and mustard. Spread over scones and bake at 220°C (425°F/Gas 7) for 12-15 minutes, or until golden.

## MEAT TIPS

✧ Nick the edges of steaks and chops with a sharp knife before cooking, to prevent the meat curling during cooking.

✧ When pan cooking meat, use a high heat to seal each side then reduce heat to medium for the rest of the cooking. Drain off any fat as it accumulates, to prevent spattering.

✧ A simple sauce can be made after pan cooking meat, by adding a little wine or stock to the pan juices. Add some garlic or spring onions (shallots) if desired and thicken with a little cornflour blended with water.

✧ Pack steaks and chops for freezing so they can be removed singly for cooking from frozen state. Use a high heat to thaw meat and seal each side, then complete cooking on medium heat.

✧ When searing smaller pieces of meat cook in small batches, as overcrowding the pan will cause the meat to stew in its own juices and become tough.

*Casserole Dish from The Bay Tree*

# Take a schnitzel

When you are pan cooking, veal needs to be protected against moisture loss and dryness. You can do this by coating it with a flour and crumb mixture.

## CRISPY COATINGS

Coatings protect the meat during cooking, and add texture and flavour. You might like to try ground nuts, crushed cornflakes, crushed chips, rolled oats, bran, sesame seeds and packaged stuffings. You will require flour, egg and your choice of coating ingredient.

**Flour:** Plain flour is used and can be seasoned with any powdered flavouring, such as paprika or curry powder. Use flour sparingly, a simple guideline is 30 g (1 oz) flour to 250 g (1/2 lb) meat. The easiest way to apply flour, is to place flour and seasonings in a freezer bag. Pat meat dry with absorbent paper and place in the bag, one piece at a time. Shake the bag until the meat is completely coated with flour, then remove meat from bag, shaking off excess flour.

**The egg:** Food is dipped into egg to provide a surface for the coating to stick to. Egg is a high protein food which coagulates when it comes in contact with heat, forming a moisture-proof barrier around the food and enclosing the natural juices. The egg is lightly beaten and usually diluted with a tablespoon of milk. The diluted mixture adheres more readily to the food.

**The coating:** This is pressed onto the egg-dipped food until the entire surface is covered. You can store any leftover coating in an airtight container for use at a later date. You might like to add herbs and grated cheese for extra flavour.

❖

## TROPICAL BANANA AND COCONUT ESCALOPES

Serves 4

- ☐ **4 lean, thin veal escalopes**
- ☐ **oil for cooking**

COATING
- ☐ **2 eggs, lightly beaten**
- ☐ **2 large bananas, mashed**
- ☐ **1/2 teaspoon ground allspice**
- ☐ **75 g (2 1/2 oz) macadamia nuts, finely chopped**
- ☐ **4 tablespoons shredded coconut**
- ☐ **30 g (1 oz) crushed cornflakes**
- ☐ **plain flour**

SPICY BROWN SAUCE
- ☐ **125 g (4 oz) crunchy peanut butter**
- ☐ **3 teaspoons brown sugar**
- ☐ **1 tablespoon Benedictine**
- ☐ **250 mL (8 fl oz) water**
- ☐ **1 clove garlic, crushed**
- ☐ **1 teaspoon grated fresh root ginger**
- ☐ **2 teaspoons curry powder**
- ☐ **1 teaspoon chilli sauce or to taste**
- ☐ **2 tablespoons single cream**

1   To make coating, combine egg, banana and allspice and set aside. Mix together nuts, coconut and cornflakes. Coat meat with flour, dip in banana mixture and coat with nut mixture. Refrigerate for 30 minutes.
2   To make sauce, place peanut butter, sugar, Benedictine, water, garlic, ginger, curry powder and chilli sauce in a saucepan and heat through over a low heat. Remove from heat and stir in cream.
3   Heat oil in a frypan. Cook escalopes for 3-4 minutes each side, or until golden brown. Remove from pan and drain on absorbent kitchen paper. Spoon sauce over and serve immediately.

❖

## CHEESY ESCALOPES WITH GINGERED CITRUS SAUCE

Serves 4

- ☐ **4 lean, thin veal escalopes**
- ☐ **oil for cooking**

*Tropical Banana and Coconut Escalopes, Cheesy Escalopes with Gingered Citrus Sauce, Veal and Avocado Rolls*

## COATING
- ☐ **125 g (4 oz) crushed cheese-flavoured cracker biscuits**
- ☐ **2 teaspoons dried chives**
- ☐ **2 teaspoons dried onion flakes**
- ☐ **plain flour**
- ☐ **1 egg, lightly beaten**

## GINGERED CITRUS SAUCE
- ☐ **315 mL (10 fl oz) double cream or evaporated skim milk**
- ☐ **1 tablespoon ginger wine**
- ☐ **2 tablespoons dry white wine**
- ☐ **1 teaspoon grated orange peel**
- ☐ **1 teaspoon grated lime peel**
- ☐ **1 tablespoon lime juice**
- ☐ **1 tablespoon orange juice**
- ☐ **1 tablespoon finely chopped preserved ginger**
- ☐ **2 egg yolks, lightly beaten**

1   To make coating, combine crushed biscuits, chives and onion flakes. Coat meat with flour, dip in egg and coat with biscuit mixture.

2   Heat oil in a frypan, cook escalopes two at a time, over a medium heat for 3-4 minutes each side, or until golden brown. Set aside and keep warm. Drain oil from pan and wipe with absorbent kitchen paper.

3   To make sauce, place cream, ginger wine, wine, orange peel, lime peel, lime juice, orange juice and ginger in pan. Bring to the boil, then reduce heat and simmer uncovered for 10 minutes. Remove from heat and whisk in egg yolks. Stir over a low heat until sauce thickens. Place meat on a serving plate, spoon sauce over and serve.

❖

# VEAL AND AVOCADO ROLLS

Serves 4

- ☐ **4 large, thin veal escalopes**
- ☐ **oil for cooking**

## STUFFING
- ☐ **30 g (1 oz) butter**
- ☐ **1 leek, finely sliced**
- ☐ **1 tablespoon chopped fresh basil**
- ☐ **1 teaspoon finely chopped fresh rosemary**
- ☐ **1 teaspoon grated lemon peel**
- ☐ **1 avocado, peeled, seeded and finely chopped**
- ☐ **60 g (2 oz) fresh breadcrumbs**

## COATING
- ☐ **1 tablespoon sesame seeds**
- ☐ **1 teaspoon grated lemon peel**
- ☐ **125 g (4 oz) dried breadcrumbs**
- ☐ **plain flour**
- ☐ **3 eggs, lightly beaten**

## PORT WINE SAUCE
- ☐ **125 mL (4 fl oz) chicken stock**
- ☐ **3 tablespoons port wine**
- ☐ **2 teaspoons cornflour blended with 3 tablespoons single cream**

1   Pound meat lightly with a mallet. Cut each escalopes in half across the grain.

2   To make stuffing, melt butter in a frypan. Cook leek for 2-3 minutes or until soft. Remove pan from heat and stir in basil, rosemary, lemon peel, avocado and breadcrumbs. Spread a heaped spoonful over each piece of meat. Roll up and secure with toothpicks.

3   To make coating, combine sesame seeds, lemon peel and breadcrumbs. Coat rolls with flour, dip into egg and roll in breadcrumb mixture. Repeat egg and breadcrumb steps. Refrigerate for 30 minutes.

4   Heat oil in a frypan, cook rolls a few at a time until golden brown and cooked through. Remove from pan and drain on absorbent kitchen paper. Set aside and keep warm.

5   To make sauce, drain oil from pan. Add stock, bring to the boil. Reduce heat and stir in port and cornflour mixture. Cook over a medium heat until sauce boils and thickens. Spoon sauce over rolls and serve.

*Coat meat with flour, then dip in egg mixture and finally in coating*

# Lamb

Lamb is one of the most versatile of meats. Almost all the cuts are prime, and therefore suitable for pan cooking and grilling. Lamb should be bright in colour, fresh in appearance with a lean cover of pale cream fat.

❖

## GLAZED MINTED LAMB RACKS

Serves 4

- ☐ **2 lean lamb racks, each containing 6 cutlets**

CRACKED WHEAT SEASONING
- ☐ **4 tablespoons cracked wheat (burghul)**
- ☐ **30 g (1 oz) fresh breadcrumbs**
- ☐ **3 tablespoons finely chopped fresh parsley**
- ☐ **1 tablespoon finely chopped fresh mint**
- ☐ **1 teaspoon grated lemon peel**
- ☐ **1 tablespoon pine nuts, toasted**
- ☐ **2 teaspoons mint jelly**
- ☐ **1 apple, peeled, cored and grated**
- ☐ **15 g ($^{1}/_{2}$ oz) butter, melted**
- ☐ **freshly ground black pepper**

MINT GLAZE
- ☐ **3 tablespoons mint jelly**
- ☐ **2 tablespoons orange juice**
- ☐ **2 tablespoons honey**

1   Using a sharp knife, separate bones from meat, leaving both ends intact, this makes a pocket for the seasoning. Trim excess fat from outside of racks.
2   To make seasoning, cover cracked wheat with boiling water and set aside to stand for 15 minutes. Drain and rinse under cold running water. Dry on absorbent kitchen paper and place in a mixing bowl with breadcrumbs, parsley, mint, lemon peel, pine nuts, mint jelly, apple, butter, and pepper to taste. Pack mixture firmly into pockets. Place racks in a baking dish.
3   To make glaze, place mint jelly in a saucepan and cook over a medium heat until melted. Stir in orange juice and honey. Brush racks with glaze and bake at 180°C (350°F/Gas 4) for 30-35 minutes or until cooked to individual taste. Baste frequently with glaze during cooking.

❖

## ROAST VEGETABLES

Serves 4

- ☐ **4 potatoes, peeled and halved**
- ☐ **4 pieces pumpkin, peeled**
- ☐ **4 brown onions, peeled**
- ☐ **1 tablespoon polyunsaturated oil**

1   Boil or steam potatoes for 5 minutes, drain and dry on absorbent kitchen paper. Set aside until cool enough to handle. Score the upper rounded side of potatoes with a fork. This helps to crisp potatoes during cooking.
2   Brush potatoes, pumpkin and onions with oil and place in baking dish and bake at 180°C (350°F/Gas 4) for about 1 hour or until golden and crisp. Remove from baking dish and keep warm.

❖

## GRAVY FROM PAN JUICES

Makes 375 mL (12 fl oz)

- ☐ **1$^{1}/_{2}$ tablespoons plain flour**
- ☐ **375 mL (12 fl oz) beef stock**
- ☐ **1 teaspoon Worcestershire sauce**

1   Drain all but 2 tablespoons of juices from baking tin. Place baking tin over heat, stir in flour and cook over a medium heat until lightly browned.
2   Remove from heat and gradually blend in stock and Worcestershire sauce. Return to heat and cook, stirring constantly until gravy boils and thickens. Strain gravy into a small saucepan and cover to prevent a skin forming. Reheat when required.

*Glazed Minted Lamb Racks with Roast Vegetables*

## Meaty Matters

**Buying meat:** The first and most important rule to follow when buying meat, is to get to know your butcher. After all, the butcher is the best person to advise you on what cuts are most suitable for your cooking needs. If you do have a bad experience with poor quality meat, don't be afraid to mention this when you are next in the store. It could be that you used the wrong cooking method for the cut of meat.

✧ When selecting meat, look for meat with a clear, but not too bright colour. Avoid meat with a greyish tinge and dried edges.

**Storing meat:** Meat should be unpacked, loosely wrapped in plastic food wrap and stored in the refrigerator or freezer as soon as possible after purchasing.

✧ If it is not frozen, offal, minced meat and thin cuts of veal should be eaten within a day or two of buying.

✧ Chops, steaks and cubed pieces can be left for two to three days in the refrigerator.

✧ Roasts will keep, refrigerated, for up to one week.

**Microwaving meat:** While some meat meals are ideal for microwave cooking others require a little care.

✧ The less tender cuts such as chuck, shin or brisket, which are usually made into stews and casseroles, should be cooked on a lower power setting.

✧ Roasting meat in the microwave is simple, if you remember a few rules.

✧ Your roast will cook more evenly if you elevate it on a microwave-safe roasting rack.

✧ If using a meat thermometer to register the internal temperature of meat, insert into thickest part of the roast avoiding any fat or bone. Do not use a conventional meat thermometer in the microwave; it must be one that is designed specifically for microwave use.

✧ The edges of the meat will cook first. To prevent these from overcooking, shield edges and high points with strips of aluminium foil when they are cooked. You should make sure that foil does not touch the walls of the microwave oven.

✧ On completion of cooking allow standing time. The internal temperature of the meat will rise slightly, completing the cooking.

✧ Wrap the meat in aluminium foil and stand the meat for 10-15 minutes.

✧ Standing time also allows the juices in the meat to settle, making carving easier.

✧ When cooking racks of lamb or crown roasts, shield the bones with aluminium foil throughout the cooking.

# Take a chop

❖
## LAMB AND VEGETABLE FILO PARCELS

Serves 4

- ☐ 8 lean lamb cutlets
- ☐ 2 cloves garlic, cut into slivers
- ☐ 2 teaspoons wholegrain mustard
- ☐ 90 g (3 oz) blue vein cheese
- ☐ 15 g (¹/₂ oz) butter, softened
- ☐ 1 teaspoon port wine
- ☐ 16 sheets filo pastry
- ☐ 3 tablespoons olive oil

VEGETABLE FILLING
- ☐ 15 g (¹/₂ oz) butter
- ☐ 4 spring onions (shallots), chopped
- ☐ 1 red pepper, finely chopped
- ☐ 8 button mushrooms, chopped
- ☐ 2 large lettuce leaves, finely shredded

1   Trim meat of all visible fat and insert a sliver of garlic between meat and bone of each cutlet. Grill cutlets each side on medium heat until just browned but not cooked through. Spread both sides of cutlets with mustard. Combine blue vein cheese, butter and port. Top each cutlet with a spoonful of cheese mixture.

2   To make vegetable filling, melt butter in a frypan and cook spring onions, pepper, mushrooms and lettuce for 2-3 minutes or until spring onions soften and lettuce wilts. Set aside to cool slightly.

3   Working with two sheets of pastry, brush between sheets with oil, fold in half, then in half again to form a square. Brush between folds with oil. Spread a little of the vegetable mixture over pastry, top with a cutlet, then top with more vegetable mixture. Fold pastry to enclose cutlet, leaving bone exposed, brush with oil and place on a baking tray.

4   Repeat with remaining pastry, cutlets and vegetable mixture. Bake at 220°C (425°F/Gas 7) for 10 minutes until golden.

❖
## LAMB WITH REDCURRANT SAUCE

Serves 4

- ☐ 4 large, lean, lamb chump chops

REDCURRANT SAUCE
- ☐ 1 tablespoon lime juice
- ☐ 125 g (4 oz) redcurrant jelly
- ☐ 2 tablespoons French mustard

1   Trim excess fat from chops. Grill, pan cook or barbecue for 4-5 minutes each side or until cooked to individual liking. Set aside and keep warm.

2   To make sauce, place lime juice, redcurrant jelly and mustard in a small saucepan and cook gently until jelly melts and all ingredients are blended. Spoon sauce over chops and serve.

❖
## LAMB AND WINTER VEGETABLE HOTPOT

Serves 4

- ☐ 2 tablespoons polyunsaturated oil
- ☐ 8 lean, lamb chump chops, meat cut into 2.5 cm (1 in) cubes
- ☐ 1 large onion, quartered
- ☐ 1 large carrot, thickly sliced
- ☐ 2 sticks celery, sliced
- ☐ 1 parsnip, sliced
- ☐ 1 small turnip, diced
- ☐ 1 potato, diced
- ☐ 60 g (2 oz) butter
- ☐ 4 tablespoons plain flour
- ☐ freshly ground black pepper
- ☐ 1 tablespoon finely chopped fresh thyme
- ☐ 1 tablespoon finely chopped fresh rosemary
- ☐ 500 mL (16 fl oz) chicken stock
- ☐ 1 tablespoon Worcestershire sauce
- ☐ 2 teaspoons soy sauce
- ☐ 2 tablespoons tomato sauce
- ☐ 125 g (4 oz) frozen peas

1   Heat oil in a large saucepan, cook meat in batches until brown on all sides. Remove from pan and set aside. Add onion to the pan and cook for 2-3 minutes, or until golden. Stir in carrot, celery, parsnip, turnip and potato. Reduce heat to low, cover and cook vegetables for 5 minutes, stirring occasionally. Remove from pan and set aside.

2   Drain oil from pan and wipe clean. Melt butter in same pan, stir in flour, pepper, thyme and rosemary and cook for 4-5 minutes, or until flour is a light straw colour.

Remove pan from heat and blend in stock, Worcestershire, soy and tomato sauces. Cook over a medium heat, stirring frequently until sauce boils and thickens.

3   Return meat and vegetables to the pan, cover and simmer gently for 1½ hours or until meat is tender.

---

### COOK'S TIP

Noisettes are rolled, boneless loin chops. The meat is rolled up tightly and tied. Most butchers are happy to prepare noisettes for you if you order them in advance.

---

❖

## LAMB WITH A TANGY APRICOT SAUCE

Serves 4

- ☐ **8 lamb noisettes**

TANGY APRICOT SAUCE
- ☐ **125 g (4 oz) apricot jam**
- ☐ **1 tablespoon soy sauce**
- ☐ **1 clove garlic, crushed**
- ☐ **½ teaspoon ground cinnamon**
- ☐ **1 tablespoon white wine vinegar**

1   Grill, pan cook or barbecue noisettes for 4-5 minutes each side or until cooked to desired liking. Set aside and keep warm.

2   To make sauce, place jam, soy sauce, garlic, cinnamon and vinegar in a small saucepan. Cook gently over a low heat until jam melts and all ingredients are blended. Spoon sauce over noisettes.

---

❖

## CRUSTY INDIVIDUAL LAMB AND KIDNEY PIES

Serves 4

FILLING
- ☐ **750 g (1½ lb) best neck chops**
- ☐ **3 lamb kidneys**
- ☐ **60 g (2 oz) butter**
- ☐ **1 onion, chopped**
- ☐ **3 bacon rashers, chopped**
- ☐ **2 tablespoons plain flour**
- ☐ **3 tablespoons red wine**
- ☐ **185 mL (6 fl oz) chicken stock**
- ☐ **1 tablespoon tomato paste**
- ☐ **½ teaspoon sugar**
- ☐ **1 tablespoon finely chopped fresh thyme**
- ☐ **freshly ground black pepper**

CRUST
- ☐ **125 g (4 oz) butter, softened**
- ☐ **315 g (10 oz) thick sour cream**
- ☐ **1 egg**
- ☐ **185 g (6 oz) self-raising flour**
- ☐ **1 tablespoon finely chopped fresh parsley**

1   Remove meat from bones and trim of all visible fat. Cut into 2.5 cm (1 in) cubes. Trim kidneys of visible fat and soak in salted water for 10 minutes. Wipe dry with absorbent kitchen paper. Nick the skin on the rounded side of each kidney and draw it back on each side until it is attached by the core only. Draw out as much core as possible and cut, with skin, close to the kidney. Cut each kidney into slices.

2   Melt 30 g (1 oz) butter in a large saucepan, cook meat in batches until browned on all sides. Remove from pan and set aside. Add kidney to the pan and cook for 1-2 minutes or until just sealed. Remove from pan and set aside. Stir in onion and bacon and cook for 2-3 minutes or until golden. Remove from pan and set aside.

3   Melt remaining butter, add flour and cook for 3-4 minutes or until a light straw colour. Blend in wine, stock, tomato paste and sugar and cook over a medium heat, stirring constantly until sauce boils and thickens. Season with thyme and pepper. Return meat mixture to the pan, cover and simmer gently for 1½ hours or until meat is tender. Set aside to cool slightly.

4   To make crust, combine butter, sour cream and egg in a bowl. Sift in 125 g (4 oz) of flour and add parsley. Mix until well combined. Divide two-thirds of mixture into four equal portions. Press each portion over base and sides of four individual dishes, and spoon in filling. Lightly knead remaining flour into remaining dough. Press out on a lightly floured surface, using palm of hand, to 1 cm (½ in) thickness and cut into rounds using a 2.5 cm (1 in) metal pastry cutter. Top filling with dough rounds, overlapping slightly. Bake at 180°C (350°F/Gas 4) for 30 minutes until golden.

*From left: Lamb with a Tangy Apricot Sauce, Lamb with Redcurrant Sauce, Lamb and Winter Vegetable Hotpot, Crusty Individual Lamb and Kidney Pies, Lamb and Vegetable Filo Parcels*

# Take some pork

Succulent pork is still one of the most popular meats. Pork should be cooked just long enough to retain its moisture and texture. If you overcook it the texture and flavour will deteriorate.

❖

## ROASTED PORK LOIN

Serves 8

- ☐ 1¹/₂ kg (3 lb) boneless pork loin
- ☐ 1 tablespoon coarse cooking salt

SEASONING
- ☐ 30 g (1 oz) butter
- ☐ 4 spinach leaves, stalks removed and leaves shredded
- ☐ 3 tablespoons pine nuts
- ☐ 30 g (1 oz) fresh breadcrumbs
- ☐ ¹/₄ teaspoon ground nutmeg
- ☐ freshly ground black pepper

CHUNKY APPLE AND PEAR SAUCE
- ☐ 1 small green apple, peeled, cored and sliced
- ☐ 1 small pear, peeled, cored and sliced
- ☐ 2 teaspoons chopped dried dates
- ☐ 4 tablespoons apple juice
- ☐ 2 teaspoons honey
- ☐ 1 teaspoon grated lemon peel
- ☐ pinch ground cloves

1   Unroll loin and make a cut in the middle of the fleshy part of the meat, making a space for the seasoning. Score the rind with a sharp knife, cutting down into the fat under the rind.
2   To make seasoning, melt butter in a frypan. Cook spinach and pine nuts for 2-3 minutes or until spinach wilts. Remove pan from heat and stir in breadcrumbs, nutmeg, and pepper to taste. Spread spinach mixture over cut flap.
3   Roll up loin firmly and secure with string. Place in a baking dish. Rub all over rind with salt and bake at 260°C (500°F/Gas 10) for 20 minutes. Reduce temperature to 180°C (350°F/Gas 4) and bake for 1 hour longer or until juices run clear when pierced in the meatiest part.
4   To make sauce, place apple, pear, dates, apple juice, honey, lemon peel and cloves in a small saucepan. Cover and bring to the boil. Reduce heat and simmer for 5 minutes, or until apple is tender.

❖

## HONEY-GLAZED PORK

Serves 4

- ☐ 500 g (1 lb) pork fillets

GLAZE
- ☐ 1 tablespoon honey
- ☐ 1 tablespoon orange juice
- ☐ 1 teaspoon light soy sauce

Trim meat of all visible fat and connective tissue. Place in a baking dish. Combine honey, orange juice and soy sauce and brush over fillets. Bake at 180°C (350°F/Gas 4) for 30 minutes. Halfway through cooking turn and brush with any leftover glaze. Slice fillets, spoon over sauce of your choice, and serve.

❖

## BANANA AND APRICOT SAUCE

- ☐ 1 banana, chopped
- ☐ 1 teaspoon lemon juice
- ☐ 425 g (14 oz) canned apricot halves
- ☐ ¹/₄ teaspoon ground cinnamon
- ☐ 2 tablespoons coconut cream

1   Place banana, lemon juice, undrained apricots, cinnamon and coconut cream in a food processor or blender and process until smooth.
2   Transfer to a small saucepan and cook gently without boiling, until heated through.

---

### BUYING PORK

When you buy pork it should be pale-fleshed with a sweet smell, not slimy or bloody. With improved technology and butchering you can now buy smaller, leaner cuts of pork – meat that is ideal for today's lifestyle.

---

*Pork Cuts*

**Loin of pork:** A loin of pork makes a great smaller roast. You can specify the number of chops you require and so avoid waste. Don't be afraid to ask your butcher to remove the bones for a boneless loin, or to score the rind. You might like to pack a boneless loin with a fruit or savoury filling.
**Butterfly pork steaks:** These steaks are cut from the mid loin area, boned, cut almost in half and opened out flat. Try placing a fruit or savoury filling on one side of the steak, then folding it over and securing with toothpicks. You can then pan cook or bake these steaks.
**Pork fillets:** Pork fillets are lean pieces of meat taken from the loin ribs. Fillets are quick and easy to cook and they have no waste. You can roast or pan cook pork fillets, then serve, sliced, with a sauce.

❖

## MUSTARD SAUCE

Serves 4

- ☐ 30 g (1 oz) butter
- ☐ 1¹/₂ tablespoons plain flour
- ☐ 2 teaspoons Dijon-style mustard
- ☐ 185 mL (6 fl oz) chicken stock
- ☐ 1 teaspoon lime juice
- ☐ freshly ground black pepper
- ☐ 3 tablespoons mayonnaise

1   Melt butter in a saucepan, stir in flour and mustard and cook for 1 minute. Remove pan from heat and blend in stock and lime juice. Season to taste.
2   Cook over a medium heat, stirring frequently until sauce boils and thickens. Remove from heat and stir in mayonnaise.

❖

## TOMATO AND PASSION FRUIT SAUCE

Serves 4

- ☐ 1 tomato, peeled, seeded and chopped
- ☐ 1 small apple, peeled, cored and grated
- ☐ 2 tablespoons orange juice
- ☐ 1 tablespoon tomato paste
- ☐ 1¹/₂ tablespoons apricot jam
- ☐ ¹/₄ teaspoon yellow mustard seeds
- ☐ pulp 2 passion fruit

Place tomato, apple, orange juice, tomato paste, jam, mustard seeds and passion fruit pulp in a saucepan. Cook over a medium heat, stirring frequently until sauce boils and all ingredients are well blended.

# PORK WITH CABBAGE AND CARAWAY SEEDS

Serves 4

- ☐ **4 large, lean, pork butterfly steaks**
- ☐ **15 g (¹/₂ oz) butter**

FILLING
- ☐ **¹/₄ savoy cabbage, finely shredded**
- ☐ **1 stick celery, finely sliced**
- ☐ **90 g (3 oz) cooked white rice**
- ☐ **1 teaspoon caraway seeds**
- ☐ **2 tablespoons thick sour cream or unflavoured yogurt**
- ☐ **freshly ground black pepper**

SAUCE
- ☐ **2 tablespoons brown sugar**
- ☐ **30 g (1 oz) butter**
- ☐ **3 tablespoons dry white wine**
- ☐ **125 mL (4 fl oz) chicken stock**
- ☐ **3 tablespoons cider vinegar**
- ☐ **¹/₂ teaspoon cornflour blended with 1 teaspoon of water**

1   Trim meat of all visible fat. Place each steak between two sheets of plastic food wrap and pound lightly with a rolling pin.

2   To make filling, boil, steam or microwave cabbage and celery, separately, until just tender. Drain and refresh under cold running water. Dry between sheets of absorbent kitchen paper.

3   Combine cabbage, celery, rice, caraway seeds, sour cream and pepper to taste. Divide mixture between steaks and spread over one half of each steak. Fold steaks over and secure with toothpicks. Melt butter in a frypan, cook steaks on both sides until golden brown. Place steaks in a baking dish and set aside. Wipe pan clean.

4   To make sauce, place sugar and butter in a pan and cook until sugar dissolves. Blend in wine, stock and vinegar and simmer for 3 minutes. Pour over steaks in baking dish. Bake uncovered at 180°C (350°F/ Gas 4) for 20-30 minutes or until tender. Baste with sauce frequently during cooking.

5   Strain sauce from pan and place in a small saucepan. Stir in cornflour mixture and heat until sauce thickens slightly. Spoon over steaks and serve.

*Top: Roasted Pork Loin*
*Centre: Honey-Glazed Pork with Banana and Apricot Sauce, Mustard Sauce, Tomato and Passion Fruit Sauce*
*Bottom: Pork with Cabbage and Caraway Seeds*

# Chicken

Childhood memories include roast chicken with a tasty stuffing. Today's busy homemaker can buy chicken cut into the right pieces for the recipe – drumsticks, fillets, breasts.

❖

## CHICKEN DRUMSTICK CASSEROLE

Serves 4

- ☐ **8 chicken drumsticks**
- ☐ **60 g (2 oz) flour**
- ☐ **3 tablespoons olive oil**
- ☐ **1 onion, sliced**
- ☐ **1 clove garlic, crushed**
- ☐ **30 g (1 oz) butter**
- ☐ **250 mL (8 fl oz) dry red wine**
- ☐ **125 mL (4 fl oz) chicken stock**
- ☐ **425 g (14 fl oz) canned tomatoes, undrained and mashed**
- ☐ **2 teaspoons finely chopped fresh rosemary**
- ☐ **250 g (8 oz) button mushrooms**
- ☐ **3 tablespoons single cream**
- ☐ **freshly ground black pepper**

1   Coat drumsticks with 4 tablespoons of flour. Heat 2 tablespoons olive oil in a large frypan, add drumsticks and brown. Remove from pan and set aside.
2   Add onion and garlic to pan and cook for 3-4 minutes or until onion softens. Add butter and melt. Stir in remaining flour and cook for 1 minute. Return chicken to pan.
3   Combine wine, stock, tomatoes and rosemary and add to pan. Bring to the boil and simmer for 30 minutes, or until drumsticks are cooked through.
4   Heat remaining oil in a small frypan and cook mushrooms for 3-4 minutes. Stir mushrooms and cream into chicken mixture. Season to taste with pepper.

### COOK'S TIP
You may wish to use a variety of chicken pieces, such as wings or thighs, with the drumsticks. If you are watching your weight, remove the skin from the chicken before cooking. Most of the fat in the chicken is found in the skin.

### IS YOUR BIRD COOKED?
✦  To test when a bird is cooked place a skewer into the thickest part of the breast and when the skewer is removed the juices should run clear. If the juices are tinged pink return to the oven and continue cooking.
✦  On completion of cooking allow whole birds to stand for 10-20 minutes. This tenderises the meat by allowing the juices to settle into the flesh.

❖

## FETA DRUMSTICKS

Serves 6

- ☐ **30 g (1 oz) butter**
- ☐ **1 clove garlic, crushed**
- ☐ **1 bunch English spinach, finely shredded**
- ☐ **2 slices ham, finely chopped**
- ☐ **125 g (4 oz) feta cheese, broken into small pieces**
- ☐ **1 teaspoon ground coriander**
- ☐ **3 teaspoons ground nutmeg**
- ☐ **freshly ground black pepper**
- ☐ **12 chicken drumsticks**
- ☐ **2 tablespoons olive oil**

1   Melt butter in a frypan, add garlic and cook for 1 minute. Stir in half the spinach and cook for 3-4 minutes, or until spinach is tender. Remove from pan and set aside. Repeat with remaining spinach.
2   Combine spinach mixture, ham, cheese, coriander and 1 teaspoon nutmeg. Season to taste with pepper. Ease skin carefully away from drumstick to form a pocket. Place a spoonful of mixture into the pocket and pull skin over. Repeat with remaining mixture and drumsticks.
3   Brush drumsticks with oil, sprinkle with remaining nutmeg and place in a baking dish. Bake at 180°C (350°F/Gas 4) for 30 minutes, or until cooked through.

Bowl from Lifestyle Imports

## TAKE A STUFFING

A stuffing transforms succulent roast chicken into something extra special. For a change, instead of placing the stuffing in the cavity of the bird try placing it between the skin and the flesh.

### BASIC BREAD STUFFING

- ☐ **125 g (4 oz) fresh breadcrumbs**
- ☐ **1 onion, finely chopped**
- ☐ **60 g (2 oz) butter, melted**
- ☐ **1 egg, lightly beaten**
- ☐ **90 g (3 oz) pine nuts, toasted**
- ☐ **2 teaspoons chopped fresh parsley**
- ☐ **1 tablespoon chopped fresh rosemary**
- ☐ **freshly ground black pepper**

Combine breadcrumbs, onion, butter, egg, pine nuts, parsley and rosemary in a bowl and mix well. Season to taste with freshly ground black pepper and use as desired.

### *Variations*

**Fruity Stuffing:** Soak 125 g (4 oz) chopped mixed fruit in 125 mL (4 fl oz) of dry white wine for 30 minutes. Mix into the basic stuffing. Fruits such as apricots, prunes and currants are popular choices. Replace the rosemary with 1 teaspoon of mixed spice.

**Ham and Mushroom Stuffing:** Add to the basic stuffing 125 g (4 oz) finely chopped ham, 90 g (3 oz) sliced button mushrooms that have been cooked in 1 teaspoon of olive oil, and 1 tablespoon French mustard.

**Hot 'n' Spicy Stuffing:** Add 1/2 teaspoon chilli powder to the basic stuffing. Replace pine nuts with the same quantity of sunflower seeds and replace parsley and rosemary with 1 teaspoon ground cumin and 1 teaspoon garam masala.

*Feta Drumsticks, Chicken Drumstick Casserole*

# Take a chicken fillet

## STRAWBERRY CHICKEN WITH PINK PEPPERCORN SAUCE

*Delicately different, this chicken fillet holds a fruity surprise and is accompanied by a subtle pepper sauce.*

Serves 4

- [ ] **4 chicken breast fillets**
- [ ] **30 g (1 oz) almonds, finely chopped**
- [ ] **125 g (4 oz) strawberries, hulled and chopped**

SAUCE
- [ ] **30 g (1 oz) butter**
- [ ] **1 tablespoon flour**
- [ ] **4 tablespoons red wine**
- [ ] **4 tablespoons milk**
- [ ] **125 mL (4 fl oz) single cream**
- [ ] **1/2 teaspoon mixed spice**
- [ ] **1 tablespoon pink peppercorns, rinsed and drained**
- [ ] **freshly ground black pepper**

1   Remove all visible fat from fillets. Place between two pieces of plastic wrap and pound with a rolling pin to flatten.
2   Sprinkle each fillet with almonds and strawberries. Fold in shorter ends of fillets and then roll up to enclose the filling. Secure with toothpicks. Place on a roasting rack in a baking dish and bake at 180°C (350°F/Gas 4) for 15-20 minutes or until fillets are cooked through.
3   To make sauce, melt butter in a small saucepan, stir in flour and cook for 1 minute. Remove from heat.
4   Combine wine, milk, cream and mixed spice and gradually stir into flour mixture. Cook over a medium heat, stirring constantly, until sauce thickens slightly. Remove from heat and add peppercorns. Season to taste with pepper and serve with chicken rolls.

*Chicken with Almonds and Herbs, Cheesy Chicken Rolls, Strawberry Chicken with Pink Peppercorn Sauce*

---

### FREEZING POULTRY
✧ Frozen poultry should not have a layer of ice around the bird. This indicates that the bird has been thawed and refrozen.
✧ Completely thaw frozen birds before cooking and make sure that all the ice crystals are removed.
✧ To thaw birds place them in the bottom of the refrigerator for 24-36 hours, or, thaw in the microwave on DEFROST (30%) for 10-15 minutes per 500 g (1 lb) of chicken.

---

## CHEESY CHICKEN ROLLS

Serves 6

- [ ] **2 tablespoons olive oil**
- [ ] **2 cloves garlic, crushed**
- [ ] **4 chicken breast fillets, cut into thin strips**
- [ ] **125 g (4 oz) button mushrooms, sliced**
- [ ] **60 g (2 oz) fresh breadcrumbs**
- [ ] **250 g (8 oz) ricotta cheese**
- [ ] **1 tablespoon chopped parsley**
- [ ] **1 tablespoon snipped chives**
- [ ] **freshly ground black pepper**
- [ ] **185 g (6 oz) prepared puff pastry, thawed**
- [ ] **1 egg, lightly beaten**

1   Heat oil in a frypan and cook garlic and chicken, in separate batches, over a medium heat for 3-5 minutes, or until chicken is cooked. Remove from pan, drain and set aside.
2   Add mushrooms and cook for 3-4 minutes. Combine chicken, mushrooms, breadcrumbs, cheese, parsley and chives. Season to taste with pepper.
3   Roll pastry out to 5 mm (1/4 in) thick and cut into four 15 x 10 cm (6 x 4 in) rectangles. Divide mixture between them. Brush edges with water and fold to form a parcel. Place on a wetted oven tray, brush with egg and bake at 180°C (350°F/Gas 4) for 30 minutes or until golden.

---

## CHICKEN WITH ALMONDS AND HERBS

*A variation on the world famous Russian Chicken Kiev, this recipe adds mustard and chopped almonds to give an interesting combination of flavours.*

Serves 4

- [ ] **4 chicken breast fillets**
- [ ] **oil for cooking**

COATING
- [ ] **60 g (2 oz) plain flour seasoned with freshly ground black pepper**
- [ ] **2 eggs, lightly beaten with 4 tablespoons milk**
- [ ] **125 g (4 oz) fresh white breadcrumbs**

HERB BUTTER
- [ ] **185 g (6 oz) butter, softened**
- [ ] **60 g (2 oz) almonds, chopped**
- [ ] **2 teaspoons French mustard**
- [ ] **1 tablespoon chopped fresh parsley**
- [ ] **1 tablespoon snipped fresh chives**
- [ ] **freshly ground black pepper**

1   To make herb butter, combine butter, almonds, mustard, parsley and chives. Season to taste with pepper. Divide mixture into four portions and shape into rolls 10 cm long. Refrigerate until firm.
2   Remove all visible fat from fillets. Place between two pieces of plastic food wrap and pound with a rolling pin to flatten. Take care not to put a hole in the flesh or the butter will run out during cooking.
3   Place a butter roll in the centre of each chicken breast. Fold the shorter ends of the fillets into the centre and then roll up to fully encase the butter. Secure fillets with toothpicks.
4   To coat, roll fillets in flour, dip in egg mixture and roll in breadcrumbs. Repeat egg and breadcrumb steps. Cover and refrigerate for 1 hour
5   Heat oil in a large saucepan and cook chicken for 5-8 minutes or until golden brown and cooked through.

---

### COOK'S TIP
Do not allow the oil to become too hot when cooking crumbed foods or the coating will brown before the chicken is cooked.

# Seafood

In these health-conscious times, fish is becoming increasingly popular. It is low in fat and high in protein, quick and easy to cook and perfect for microwaving.

## THAI FISH

*These grilled fish with their spicy flavour are sure to become a favourite.*

Serves 4

- [ ] 4 small whole fish

MARINADE
- [ ] 2 small red chillies, seeded and finely chopped
- [ ] 1 clove garlic, crushed
- [ ] 2 teaspoons grated root ginger
- [ ] 1 1/2 tablespoons chopped fresh coriander
- [ ] 2 tablespoons lime juice
- [ ] 2 tablespoons peanut oil
- [ ] 1 teaspoon ground cumin
- [ ] freshly ground black pepper

1  Rinse fish under cold running water and pat dry with absorbent kitchen paper. Score flesh with a sharp knife to make 2-3 diagonal cuts along the body. Place in a shallow dish.
2  To make marinade, combine chilli, garlic, ginger, coriander, lime juice, oil and cumin in a small bowl. Season to taste with pepper. Pour over fish and rub well into the flesh. Cover and marinate for 2 hours, or preferably overnight in the refrigerator.
3  Remove fish from marinade and grill under a medium heat for 8-10 minutes, or until fish flakes when tested with a fork. Baste frequently with marinade and turn halfway through cooking.

---
### COOK'S TIP
✧  These tasty fish are also great barbecued or pan cooked.
✧  Fish is cooked when it flakes easily when tested with a fork; if it is overcooked it will be dry and tough.
---

*Spicy Seafood Cakes, Baked Stuffed Fish, Thai Fish*

## BAKED STUFFED FISH

*Bream has been used for this recipe, however any whole fish, such as snapper or emperor, is suitable.*

Serves 4

- [ ] 1 tablespoon olive oil
- [ ] 1 small onion, finely chopped
- [ ] 1 clove garlic, crushed
- [ ] 3 spinach leaves, stalks removed and leaves finely shredded
- [ ] 2 bacon rashers, finely chopped
- [ ] 2 tablespoons currants
- [ ] 2 tablespoons pine nuts, toasted
- [ ] 60 g (2 oz) fresh breadcrumbs
- [ ] 1 egg, lightly beaten
- [ ] 2 teaspoons lemon juice
- [ ] 1 tablespoon chopped fresh parsley
- [ ] 1 tablespoon chopped fresh rosemary
- [ ] freshly ground black pepper
- [ ] 2 whole fish, about 500 g (1 lb) each, cleaned and scaled
- [ ] 250 mL (8 fl oz) dry white wine
- [ ] 60 g (2 oz) butter, melted

1  Heat oil in a non-stick frypan and cook onion and garlic for 3-4 minutes or until onion softens. Add spinach and bacon and cook for 5 minutes longer, or until spinach wilts. Remove from heat.
2  Combine spinach mixture, currants, pine nuts, breadcrumbs, egg, lemon juice, parsley and rosemary in a large bowl. Season to taste with pepper and mix well.
3  Divide mixture into two portions and fill the cavities of each fish. Close securely, using skewers or toothpicks. Place in a greased shallow baking dish, pour wine over and brush fish with butter.
4  Bake at 180°C (350°F/Gas 4) for 35-40 minutes, or until fish flakes when tested with a fork. Baste frequently during cooking.

## SPICY SEAFOOD CAKES

Serves 4

- [ ] 500 g (1 lb) potatoes, peeled and chopped
- [ ] 250 mL (8 fl oz) water
- [ ] 2 lime leaves
- [ ] 155 g (5 oz) uncooked prawns, shelled and deveined
- [ ] 100 g (3 1/2 oz) scallops
- [ ] 250 g (8 oz) white fish fillets
- [ ] 60 g (2 oz) grated tasty cheese
- [ ] 2 tablespoons flour
- [ ] 2 eggs, lightly beaten
- [ ] 1 tablespoon lemon juice
- [ ] 2 tablespoons lime juice
- [ ] 2 teaspoons grated lemon peel
- [ ] 1 small red chilli, seeded and finely chopped
- [ ] 1 tablespoon finely chopped fresh coriander
- [ ] freshly ground black pepper to taste
- [ ] 125 g (4 oz) dried breadcrumbs
- [ ] oil for cooking

PLUM SAUCE
- [ ] 4 tablespoons fruit chutney, large pieces chopped
- [ ] 125 g (4 oz) plum jam
- [ ] 1 tablespoon red wine vinegar
- [ ] 1 teaspoon Chinese five spice

1  Boil, steam or microwave potatoes until tender. Drain well and mash.
2  Place water and lime leaves into a frypan and heat over a medium heat until simmering. Reduce heat, add prawns and scallops and cook for 2-3 minutes or until prawns just change colour. Remove seafood from liquid and drain on absorbent kitchen paper. Place in a food processor or blender and process until smooth.
3  Bring liquid back to the simmer and cook fish for 10-15 minutes, or until it flakes when tested with a fork. Remove pan from heat and allow fish to cool in the liquid. When cool, remove from pan and flake with a fork.
4  Combine potato, prawn mixture, fish, cheese, flour, eggs, lemon and lime juices, lemon peel, chilli and coriander in a large bowl and mix well. Season to taste with pepper. Shape mixture into eight patties, coat with breadcrumbs and refrigerate for 30 minutes.
5  Heat oil in a frypan, cook patties until golden brown on each side. Drain on absorbent kitchen paper.
6  To make sauce, place chutney, jam, vinegar and five spice in saucepan. Bring to the boil, stirring constantly, and simmer for 5 minutes. Serve with seafood cakes.

*Glass platter from HAG, Plates from Studio HAUS*

# Take a fish cutlet

A cutlet is a cross-sectional slice of a fish. In the following recipes the cutlets are pan cooked and served with the sauce of your choice.

❖

## FISH CUTLETS WITH ONE OF THREE SAUCES

Serves 4

☐ **1 tablespoon olive oil**
☐ **30 g (1 oz) butter**
☐ **4 fish cutlets**

Heat oil and butter in a large nonstick frypan. Cook cutlets over a medium heat for 3-5 minutes, or until fish flakes with a fork, turning once during cooking.

❖

## CREAMY APRICOT SAUCE

☐ **155 g (5 oz) canned apricots, drained and chopped**
☐ **45 g ($1^1/2$ oz) blanched almonds, chopped**
☐ **125 g (4 oz) ricotta cheese**
☐ **1 tablespoon dry sherry**
☐ **125 mL (4 fl oz) single cream**
☐ **2 teaspoons Grand Marnier**
☐ **1 tablespoon lemon juice**
☐ **freshly ground black pepper**

1  Place apricots, almonds, ricotta and sherry in a food processor or blender and process until smooth. Stir in cream and Grand Marnier.
2  Transfer mixture to a small saucepan and heat through. Stir in lemon juice and season to taste with pepper.

❖

## TARTARE SAUCE

☐ **250 mL (8 fl oz) mayonnaise**
☐ **2 tablespoons finely chopped gherkin**
☐ **1 tablespoon chopped capers**
☐ **2 teaspoons finely chopped fresh parsley**
☐ **1 teaspoon chopped fresh dill**

Combine mayonnaise, gherkin, capers, parsley and dill in a bowl and mix well.

## SPICY SEAFOOD SAUCE

- ☐ 30 g (1 oz) butter
- ☐ 2 tablespoons plain flour
- ☐ 250 mL (4 fl oz) chicken stock
- ☐ 250 mL (4 fl oz) milk
- ☐ 1 teaspoon Worcestershire sauce
- ☐ 3 drops Tabasco sauce
- ☐ 1 tablespoon single cream
- ☐ 1¹/₂ tablespoons tomato paste
- ☐ 60 g (2 oz) mussels meat, chopped
- ☐ 100 g (3¹/₂ oz) prawns, shelled and deveined
- ☐ 2 teaspoons chopped fresh parsley
- ☐ 2 tablespoons lemon juice
- ☐ 1 tablespoon mayonnaise
- ☐ freshly ground black pepper

1   Melt butter in a saucepan. Stir in flour and cook for 1 minute. Remove from heat and gradually whisk in stock and milk. Return to heat, stirring constantly until mixture boils and thickens.

2   Add Worcestershire sauce, Tabasco, cream, tomato paste, mussels, prawns, parsley, lemon juice and mayonnaise and heat through. Season to taste with pepper.

*Fish Cutlets with Creamy Apricot Sauce, Spicy Seafood Sauce, Tartare Sauce*

---

## MICROWAVE IT

✧ Fish and the microwave are perfect partners. The easiest way to cook fish in the microwave is to place the required number of fish fillets in a shallow microwave-safe dish, sprinkle with lemon juice and chopped fresh herbs of your choice and season with freshly ground black pepper. Cover with microwave-safe plastic food wrap and cook on HIGH (100%) for 4-5 minutes per 500 g (1 lb) of fish.

✧ Whole fish cooks well in the microwave – their eyes should be removed before cooking as they will explode. Whole fish is best cooked on a MEDIUM-HIGH (70%) power setting, allowing 5-6 minutes per 500g (1 lb) of fish.

✧ When cooking shellfish in the microwave, use a MEDIUM-HIGH (70%) power setting, or cook them in a liquid or sauce. Shellfish have a high moisture content and tend to 'pop' during cooking and will easily overcook if care is not taken. One of the easiest ways to cook shellfish is to make your sauce or heat the liquid then drop the fish in. Only a very short cooking time is then required.

---

*Storing fish*

**Whole fish, cutlets and fillets:** Wash under cold running water and dry well with absorbent kitchen paper. Place in covered container or wrap in foil and store in refrigerator. Whole fish will keep for 2-3 days. Cutlets and fillets will keep approximately 1-2 days

**Shellfish:** Place in a covered container and refrigerate and use within 1-2 days. Before storing mussels and pipis, prepare by removing beard and scrubbing shells under cold running water. If storing live molluscs, such as mussels, pipis, oysters or cockles, do not refrigerate, as this causes them to die. They are best stored in a slightly damp hessian bag in a cool, dark place. They can be stored in this way for up to 3 days in cool weather. Before cooking, discard any that have opened.

*Freezing fish*

✧ Freeze only the freshest fish.

✧ Freeze whole fish only if you intend to cook it whole; thawed fish is difficult to fillet. Ensure that all portions to be frozen are clean. Wrap in plastic wrap, or seal in a freezer bag. Name and date, then freeze.

✧ Dip the fish in cold water as soon as it is frozen and return to the freezer. This will form an ice seal which helps prevent the fish from becoming dry and 'off' flavours developing.

✧ White fish can be frozen for 4-6 months.

✧ Oily fish, such as salmon, trout and mackerel, should not be frozen for longer then 2 months.

✧ Fish is best cooked in its frozen state. On thawing it loses a large proportion of its natural juices and flavour. As fish only takes a short time to cook you do not have to worry about the problems associated with cooking frozen meats and poultry.

---

## COURT BOUILLON
*This liquid is used for poaching fish.*

- ☐ 1 litre (32 fl oz) water
- ☐ 1 stick celery, chopped
- ☐ 1 carrot, chopped
- ☐ 4 tablespoons white wine vinegar
- ☐ 1 bay leaf
- ☐ 6 peppercorns
- ☐ sprig fresh thyme

Place water, celery, carrot, vinegar, bay leaf, peppercorns and thyme in a medium saucepan. Bring to the boil and simmer for 15-20 minutes. Strain liquid and use as desired.

*Spoons from The Bay Tree*

# Take a potato

The humble potato is a meal in itself when baked and filled with a tasty stuffing, or it is a nutritious vegetable accompaniment roasted, boiled, mashed, or cooked as chips.

## THE PERFECT CHIP

*Double-cooking chips ensures crisp golden chips every time. The high water content of potatoes initially reduces the temperature of the oil and double-cooking overcomes this problem. A wire chip basket makes it easier to lower and raise a quantity of chips in hot oil. If cooking a large quantity of chips, cook in batches to prevent overcrowding.*

Serves 4

- [ ] **4 large potatoes, peeled and washed**
- [ ] **oil for cooking**

1  Cut potatoes into 1 cm slices, then into strips. Soak strips in cold water for 10 minutes to remove the excess starch. Drain and dry on absorbent kitchen paper.
2  Heat oil in a deep saucepan. Drop a chip into the oil and when it rises to the surface surrounded by bubbles the oil is at the correct temperature for cooking. Drop the chips gradually into the hot oil, or lower them in a wire basket and cook for 6 minutes.
3  Remove chips from oil using a slotted spoon, or by lifting the basket, and drain on absorbent kitchen paper. At this point the chips are blanched and can be left for several hours, or frozen before the final cooking stage.
4  Just prior to serving, reheat the oil and test as above. Cook chips quickly for 3-4 minutes or until golden brown and crisp. Remove from pan with a slotted spoon, drain on absorbent kitchen paper. Season to taste and serve immediately.

❖

## BAKED JACKET POTATOES

*Baked potatoes can be placed in the oven and cooked with other dishes. If the other food you are cooking requires a slightly lower or higher temperature your baked potatoes will happily cook along with it taking just a little shorter or longer time as the case may be.*

Serves 4

- [ ] **4 potatoes**
- [ ] **thick sour cream or butter**

Scrub and dry potatoes. Prick with a fork and place on a roasting rack in a baking dish. Bake at 180°C (350°F/Gas 4) for 1 hour or until tender. Serve with sour cream or butter.

❖

## BACON AND CREAMED CORN FILLED POTATOES

*You will require only half the potato flesh for this recipe. Reserve the remaining flesh for another use. Leftover potato can be made into potato cakes or croquettes, or can be pan cooked.*

Serves 4

- [ ] **4 potatoes, baked in their jackets**
- [ ] **4 bacon rashers, chopped**
- [ ] **125 g (4 oz) canned creamed corn**
- [ ] **2 tablespoons thick sour cream**
- [ ] **pinch chilli powder**
- [ ] **60 g (2 oz) grated tasty cheese**

1  Cut potatoes in half, scoop out flesh, leaving a 1 cm thick shell. Reserve the flesh and set aside.
2  Cook the bacon in a non-stick frypan for 2-3 minutes or until crisp. Mash half the potato flesh and combine with bacon, corn, sour cream and chilli powder. Spoon mixture into potato shells, top with cheese.
3  Place potatoes on an oven tray and bake at 180°C (350°F/Gas 4) for 15 minutes or until cheese melts.

## PERFECT ROAST POTATOES

*When roasting vegetables use a shallow baking dish, which will allow the vegetables to brown evenly. Other vegetables can be roasted with the potatoes. Cook pumpkin with or without the skin and cut into a similar size as the potatoes. Brown onions are excellent roasted; peel away 1 or 2 layers of skin, leaving a little of the root end intact to hold onions together.*

- [ ] **4 potatoes, peeled and halved**
- [ ] **1 tablespoon polyunsaturated oil**

1  Boil or steam potatoes for 5 minutes. Drain and dry on absorbent kitchen paper. Set aside until cool enough to handle, then cut in half lengthwise. Score the upper rounded surface with a fork; this helps crisp the potatoes during cooking.
2  Brush potatoes with oil and place in a shallow baking dish. Bake at 180°C (350°F/Gas 4) for 55-60 minutes, turn occasionally during cooking.

❖

## POTATO AND BEETROOT FLAN

*This vibrantly coloured dish will give any meal a lift. It may be served either hot or cold.*

Serves 4

- [ ] **4 potatoes, cooked and mashed (without milk or butter)**
- [ ] **1 large raw beetroot, grated**
- [ ] **1 tablespoon finely chopped fresh dill**
- [ ] **1 tablespoon single cream**
- [ ] **1 tablespoon mayonnaise**
- [ ] **2 teaspoons horseradish cream**
- [ ] **freshly ground black pepper**
- [ ] **2 eggs, separated**

1  Combine potatoes, beetroot, dill, cream, mayonnaise, horseradish, pepper and egg yolks in a mixing bowl.
2  Whisk egg whites until stiff peaks form and fold through potato mixture. Spoon mixture into a well-greased 23 cm (9 in) flan dish with a removable base. Bake at 200°C (400°F/Gas 6) for 25-30 minutes or until firm. Serve warm, or at room temperature, cut into wedges.

## BACON AND BANANA POTATO CAKES

Serves 4

☐ **4 potatoes, cooked and mashed (without milk or butter)**
☐ **1 small green apple, grated**
☐ **1 tablespoon mayonnaise**
☐ **2 teaspoons chopped fresh mint**
☐ **3 tablespoons plain flour**

FILLING
☐ **4 bacon rashers, finely chopped**
☐ **1 banana, sliced**

COATING
☐ **plain flour**
☐ **1 egg, lightly beaten**
☐ **125 g (4 oz) dried breadcrumbs**
☐ **oil for cooking**

1   Combine potato, apple, mayonnaise, mint and flour. Divide potato mixture into sixteen equal portions and form into patties.
2   To make filling, cook bacon in a non-stick frypan for 2-3 minutes or until crisp. Set aside to cool slightly. Place a spoonful of bacon on eight of the patties. Top with banana slices and remaining potato patties. Mould potato patties to completely seal filling.
3   To coat, cover patties lightly with flour, dip in egg then breadcrumbs. Refrigerate for 30 minutes.
4   Heat oil in a frypan and cook patties, two at a time, until golden brown on both sides. Remove from pan and drain on absorbent kitchen paper. Set aside and keep warm. Cook remaining patties.

---

### PERFECT MASHED POTATO
Serves 4

☐ **4 potatoes, peeled and halved**
☐ **125 mL (4 fl oz) milk**
☐ **30 g (1 oz) butter, softened**

1   Place potatoes in a saucepan of water, cover and bring to the boil. Cook gently for 20 minutes or until tender.
2   Drain potatoes, then return to pan. Shake pan over low heat to dry. Mash potatoes with a vegetable masher until free of lumps.
3   Stir in milk and butter. Season to taste and beat with a fork until smooth and fluffy.

---

*Top: Potato and Beetroot Flan*
*Centre: Baked Jacket Potatoes, Bacon and Creamed Corn Filled Potatoes*
*Bottom: Bacon and Banana Potato Cakes*

Plate from Studio HAUS

Plate from Studio HAUS

# Saucy vegetables

Fresh vegetables, cooked or raw, are the tastiest and healthiest foods you can eat. Try new recipes or your favourite vegetables topped with a delicious sauce.

❖
## BASIC WHITE SAUCE

*Sauces are the perfect accompaniment for vegetables. The following Basic White Sauce recipe and its variations can be served with many different steamed, boiled or microwaved vegetables.*

Makes 250 mL (8 fl oz)

- ☐ **30 g (1 oz) butter**
- ☐ **2 tablespoons plain flour**
- ☐ **¼ teaspoon dry mustard**
- ☐ **250 mL (8 fl oz) milk**

1 Melt butter in a saucepan, stir in flour and mustard. Cook over medium heat for 1 minute.

2 Remove pan from heat and whisk in milk a little at a time until well blended. Cook over medium heat, stirring constantly until sauce boils and thickens.

*Variations:*

**Cheese Sauce:** When the sauce thickens, remove from heat and stir in 60 g (2 oz) grated tasty cheese. Serve immediately. Avoid reheating after the cheese is added or it becomes tough and stringy.

## CAULIFLOWER AU GRATIN
Use Cheese Sauce and make a vegetable au gratin. For example, place steamed cauliflower in an oven-proof dish; pour sauce over. Top with grated cheese and bake at 180°C (350°F/Gas 4) for 15-20 minutes.

**Mushroom Sauce:** Melt the butter and cook 100 g (3½ oz) sliced button mushrooms for 4–5 minutes. Remove mushrooms from pan and set aside. Continue making as for Basic White Sauce, replacing 3 tablespoons of milk with cream. When sauce thickens, return mushrooms to the pan and heat through.

**Mustard Sauce:** Blend 2 teaspoons of dry mustard and 1 tablespoon sugar into the flour mixture. When sauce thickens stir in 1 tablespoon white vinegar.

**Herb Sauce:** When sauce thickens remove from heat and stir in 2 tablespoons finely chopped fresh parsley, 1 tablespoon finely snipped chives and 1 tablespoon finely chopped dill.

**Curry Sauce:** Blend 2 teaspoons of curry powder into the flour mixture and cook as for Basic White Sauce.

## THE PERFECT DRESSING

### VINAIGRETTE

Makes 250 mL (8 fl oz)

- ☐ **1 tablespoon French mustard**
- ☐ **3 tablespoons white wine vinegar**
- ☐ **freshly ground black pepper**
- ☐ **185 mL (6 fl oz) olive oil**

Place mustard in a bowl and whisk in the vinegar. Season to taste with pepper. Add the oil a little at a time, whisking well until mixture thickens.

### MAYONNAISE

Makes 500 mL (16 fl oz)

- ☐ **3 egg yolks**
- ☐ **1 tablespoon Dijon-style mustard**
- ☐ **freshly ground black pepper**
- ☐ **2 tablespoons lemon juice**
- ☐ **500 mL (16 fl oz) olive oil**

Place egg yolks, mustard, pepper to taste and lemon juice in a food processor or blender and process for 1 minute. With the machine running, add the oil in a slow, steady stream. When all of the oil is incorporated, scrape down the sides of the bowl. Transfer mixture to a glass bowl, cover and refrigerate until required.

## Vegetable preparation

✧ Vegetables need little preparation and where possible you should scrub rather than peel them. Many important vitamins are contained just under the skin.

✧ As many of the nutrients in vegetables are water soluble they are lost if the vegetables are soaked for a long time.

✧ Wash vegetables under cold running water just long enough to remove any dirt. Prepare and cook them immediately.

✧ Once cut and exposed to the air the goodness rapidly disappears.

✧ Cook vegetables in a minimal amount of water for a short time; this will keep vitamin loss to a minimum.

✧ Steaming or microwaving retains the most nutrients, as the cooking time is short and a minimal quantity of water is used.

✧ If boiling vegetables, the rule is to cook root vegetables in cold water with the lid on, and plunge green vegetables into hot water and cook with the lid off; then refresh under cold water to retain the colour and stop the cooking.

✧ An easy and tasty idea for serving hot vegetables, is to toss them in a vinaigrette dressing. Try using different vinegars, or lemon juice. Herb and fruit vinegars are all popular alternatives.

## Buying and storing vegetables

✧ Vegetables are at their best when first picked.

✧ When you are buying vegetables, choose produce without blemishes, bruises or marks.

✧ Most vegetables are best stored in the vegetable section of the refrigerator.

✧ Store tuber-type vegetables, such as potatoes, in a dry dark place like a pantry cupboard.

✧ The storage time of vegetables will greatly depend on their condition when purchased.

✧ Cover cut vegetables with plastic food wrap to prevent vitamin loss, keep the surface moist and prevent aromas in the refrigerator.

## NUTRITIOUS VEGETABLES

✧ Some of the important nutrients contained in vegetables are vitamin A, vitamin B, vitamin C, potassium, iron and magnesium. Vegetables also provide dietary fibre and complex carbohydrates.

✧ When compared by weight the vegetable which is lowest in kilojoules (calories) is celery, followed closely by cucumber and lettuce. Three long sticks of celery, twenty lettuce leaves, or half a cucumber, contain the same kilojoules as half a slice of bread.

# Take a leaf

What goes into a salad to make it green? Nowadays there are many tasty greens available to make your salads something special.

## ❖ ENDIVE, COS, TUNA AND OLIVE SALAD

Serves 4

- ☐ 1 bunch curly endive, leaves separated and washed
- ☐ 1 cos lettuce, leaves separated and washed
- ☐ 125 g (4 oz) cherry tomatoes
- ☐ 155 g (5 oz) green beans, trimmed and blanched
- ☐ 8 baby new potatoes, cooked and halved
- ☐ 3 hard-boiled eggs, quartered
- ☐ 4 spring onions (shallots), chopped
- ☐ 1/2 red pepper, cut into thin strips
- ☐ 1/2 green pepper, cut into thin strips
- ☐ 12 black olives
- ☐ 425 g (14 oz) canned tuna, drained and flaked
- ☐ 3 tablespoons finely chopped parsley

DRESSING
- ☐ 1 clove garlic, crushed
- ☐ 4 anchovy fillets, drained
- ☐ freshly ground black pepper
- ☐ 1/4 teaspoon sugar
- ☐ 2 teaspoons finely chopped fresh basil
- ☐ 2 tablespoons cider vinegar
- ☐ 4 tablespoons olive oil

1 Arrange endive and cos lettuce in a large salad bowl. Combine tomatoes, beans, potatoes, eggs, spring onions, red and green peppers, olives, tuna and parsley, and arrange attractively over lettuce.

2 To make dressing, place garlic, anchovies, pepper, sugar, basil, vinegar and oil in a food processor or blender and process until all ingredients are combined. Pour over salad and serve.

## ❖ BLUE CHEESE AND WALDORF SALAD

Serves 6

- ☐ 90 g (3 oz) blue cheese, crumbled
- ☐ 125 g (4 oz) pecan nuts, chopped
- ☐ 1 red apple, cored and thinly sliced
- ☐ 1 green apple, cored and thinly sliced
- ☐ 1 stick celery, sliced
- ☐ 1 radicchio, leaves separated and washed
- ☐ bunch watercress

DRESSING
- ☐ 2 teaspoons Dijon-style mustard
- ☐ 2 tablespoons red wine vinegar
- ☐ 1 tablespoon port wine
- ☐ 125 mL (4 fl oz) grapeseed oil

1 Combine cheese, pecans, red and green apples and celery in a bowl. Line a salad bowl with radicchio leaves and watercress and refrigerate.

2 To make dressing, combine mustard, vinegar, port and oil in a screwtop jar. Shake to combine all ingredients. Pour half the dressing over apple mixture and toss. Spoon apple salad over leaves then pour remaining dressing over and serve.

*Endive, Cos, Tuna and Olive Salad, Beetroot and Fennel Parcels, Blue Cheese and Waldorf Salad, Three Grains with Spinach and Chicken*

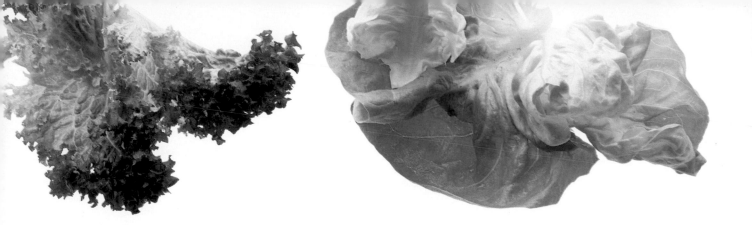

## KNOWING YOUR GREENS

**Chicory or Witloof:** Tightly clustered, smooth white leaves with yellow tips. Slightly bitter flavour.

**Curly Endive:** Sold in large bunches. The long leaves graduate from pale, greeny yellow to dark green. Use only the paler heart and stalks. Bitter flavour.

**Butter or Round lettuce:** Soft, smallish lettuce. Mild flavour.

**Cos or Romaine lettuce:** Elongated head of dark green oval leaves and a crisp pale green heart. Has a pungent flavour and stays crisp.

**Iceberg or Crisp Head lettuce:** A large lettuce with crisp outer leaves and a firm, sweet heart. The basis of many salads as the leaves stay crisp.

**Oak-leaf lettuce:** Soft, smallish leaves with edges tinged pink to red.

**Radicchio:** Beetroot-coloured with white veins and tightly packed heads.

**Rocket:** Small, acidic, dark green leaves. It is sold while the plant is still very young.

**English spinach**: Dark green leaves. Eaten raw in salads when leaves are young and fresh.

**Watercress:** Use only young outer leaves and tender stems for salads. The remainder can be used in soups. Pungent, slightly peppery flavour.

❖

## BEETROOT AND FENNEL PARCELS

Serves 4

- ☐ 8 large lettuce leaves
- ☐ 1 large raw beetroot, peeled and cut into thin strips
- ☐ 1 fennel bulb, cut into thin strips
- ☐ 1 red onion, sliced

DRESSING
- ☐ 200 g (6$^1$/2 oz) sour cream
- ☐ 4 anchovy fillets, drained
- ☐ 2 tablespoons white wine vinegar
- ☐ 1 tablespoon finely chopped fresh basil
- ☐ 2 teaspoons olive oil
- ☐ $^1$/2 teaspoon sugar

1 Bring a large saucepan of water to the boil. Plunge lettuce leaves into boiling water. Remove pan from heat, drain and refresh lettuce under cold running water. Set aside.

2 Boil or steam beetroot and fennel, separately, for 3 minutes. Drain and refresh under cold running water. Combine beetroot and fennel with onion and divide into eight equal portions. Place one portion on each lettuce leaf and roll up firmly.

3 To make dressing, place sour cream, anchovy fillets, vinegar, basil, oil and sugar in a food processor or blender and process until smooth. Arrange parcels on a serving plate, pour over dressing and serve.

❖

## THREE GRAINS WITH SPINACH AND CHICKEN

Serves 4

- ☐ 1 litre (32 fl oz) chicken stock
- ☐ 60 g (2 oz) wild rice
- ☐ 60 g (2 oz) brown rice
- ☐ 60 g (2 oz) white rice
- ☐ 1 large spinach leaf, shredded
- ☐ 125 g (4 oz) button mushrooms, sliced
- ☐ 4 spring onions (shallots), chopped
- ☐ 1 red pepper, cut into strips
- ☐ 2 tablespoons toasted pine nuts
- ☐ 4 chicken breast fillets, cooked and sliced

DRESSING
- ☐ 125 mL (4 fl oz) coconut cream
- ☐ 1 teaspoon grated fresh root ginger
- ☐ 2 tablespoons white wine vinegar
- ☐ 2 teaspoons brown sugar
- ☐ $^1$/2 teaspoon curry powder
- ☐ $^1$/4 teaspoon turmeric

1 Place stock in a large saucepan and bring to the boil. Add wild rice and brown rice and cook for 35-40 minutes or until tender. Add white rice during the last 15 minutes of cooking. Drain and rinse.

2 Place rice in a bowl and toss with spinach, mushrooms, spring onions, pepper, pine nuts and chicken.

3 To make dressing, place coconut cream, ginger, vinegar, sugar, curry powder and turmeric in a screwtop jar. Shake well and pour over salad.

# Slaws

The cabbage family includes white and red cabbage, green savoy and Chinese cabbage. Great for the diet-conscious, cabbage is high in fibre, low in kilojoules, and an excellent source of vitamin C.

❖
## HOT COLESLAW WITH BRANDY DRESSING

Serves 4

☐ **2 bacon rashers, chopped**
☐ **$^1/_2$ medium cabbage, shredded**
☐ **2 green apples, coarsely chopped**
☐ **$^1/_2$ teaspoon nutmeg**

BRANDY DRESSING
☐ **1 clove garlic, crushed**
☐ **1 tablespoon cider vinegar**
☐ **2 tablespoons brandy**
☐ **4 tablespoons walnut oil**
☐ **freshly ground black pepper**

1  Cook bacon in a heavy-based frypan until just crisp. Add cabbage and apples and toss well. Cook for 3-4 minutes, then mix in nutmeg. Using a slotted spoon transfer to a warmed bowl and toss to combine.
2  To make dressing, combine garlic, vinegar, brandy, oil and pepper in a screwtop jar and shake well. Pour over coleslaw and serve.

*Food Processor in action*

## PINEAPPLE AND KIWI FRUIT SLAW

Serves 6

- [ ] $^1/_4$ **red cabbage, shredded**
- [ ] $^1/_2$ **Chinese cabbage, shredded**
- [ ] **425 g (14 oz) canned pineapple pieces, drained and juice reserved**
- [ ] **2 kiwi fruit, peeled and sliced**
- [ ] **1 red pepper, sliced**
- [ ] **1 green pepper, sliced**

DRESSING
- [ ] **3 tablespoons grapeseed oil**
- [ ] **2 tablespoons reserved pineapple juice**
- [ ] **3 tablespoons finely chopped fresh coriander**
- [ ] **3 tablespoons finely chopped fresh mint**

1　Combine red and Chinese cabbages, pineapple, kiwi fruit and red and green peppers in a salad bowl. Toss lightly, cover and refrigerate until required.
2　To make dressing, combine oil, juice, coriander and mint in a screwtop jar. Shake well to combine all ingredients, pour over slaw and serve.

## VEGETABLE SLAW WITH PESTO DRESSING

Serves 6

- [ ] $^1/_2$ **savoy cabbage, shredded**
- [ ] **1 large carrot, cut into thin strips**
- [ ] **4 spring onions (shallots), chopped**
- [ ] **1 stick celery, cut into thin strips**
- [ ] **8 radishes, sliced**
- [ ] **1 green pepper, cut into strips**
- [ ] **155 g (5 oz) broccoli florets, cooked**

DRESSING
- [ ] **100 g (3$^1/_2$ oz) fresh basil**
- [ ] **2 cloves garlic, crushed**
- [ ] **2 tablespoons pine nuts, toasted**
- [ ] **2 tablespoons grated Parmesan cheese**
- [ ] **5 tablespoons mayonnaise**
- [ ] **3 tablespoons unflavoured yogurt**

1　Place cabbage, carrot, spring onions, celery, radishes, pepper and broccoli in a salad bowl. Toss lightly, cover and refrigerate until required.
2　To make dressing, place basil, garlic, pine nuts, Parmesan, mayonnaise and yogurt in a food processor or blender and process until smooth. Pour dressing over slaw and toss lightly.

*Bowls and Servers from Bibelot, Laminate from Albet Laminati*

## THREE-CABBAGE HOT SLAW

Serves 6

- [ ] **1 tablespoon vegetable oil**
- [ ] **1 tablespoon sesame oil**
- [ ] **1 clove garlic, crushed**
- [ ] **1 teaspoon grated root ginger**
- [ ] **1 red chilli, seeded and chopped**
- [ ] **1 tablespoon sesame seeds**
- [ ] $^1/_4$ **red cabbage, shredded**
- [ ] $^1/_4$ **Chinese cabbage, shredded**
- [ ] $^1/_4$ **savoy cabbage, shredded**

1　Heat vegetable and sesame oils in a wok or frypan until very hot. Add garlic, ginger, chilli and sesame seeds and stir-fry for 1 minute.
2　Toss in cabbages and stir-fry for 3-4 minutes or until just cooked. The cabbages should still retain their colours and be crisp. Serve immediately.

*Pineapple and Kiwi Fruit Slaw,*
*Vegetable Slaw with Pesto Dressing,*
*Three-Cabbage Hot Slaw,*
*Hot Coleslaw with Brandy Dressing*

# Take some pasta or rice

Rice and pasta are important staple foods for much of the world's population. Reasonably bland in flavour, they combine well with many other foods.

❖

## SEAFOOD AND TOMATO SAUCE

*Any combination of seafood can be used in this sauce. For a less spicy dish you may wish to omit the chilli.*

Serves 4

- ☐ 1 tablespoon olive oil
- ☐ 4 spring onions (shallots), finely chopped
- ☐ 1 clove garlic, crushed
- ☐ 1 small red chilli, finely chopped
- ☐ 500 g (1 lb) cooked prawns, peeled, deveined and chopped
- ☐ 125 g (4 oz) scallops, halved, with coral removed
- ☐ 410 g (13 oz) canned tomatoes, undrained and mashed
- ☐ 3 tablespoons red wine
- ☐ 3 tablespoons chicken stock
- ☐ 2 teaspoons tomato paste
- ☐ 1 teaspoon sugar
- ☐ 2 teaspoons chopped fresh basil
- ☐ 1 tablespoon chopped fresh parsley
- ☐ 8 oysters in the shell

1   Heat oil in a large saucepan and cook spring onions, garlic and chilli for 1 minute. Stir in prawns and scallops and cook for 2 minutes longer.
2   Combine tomatoes, wine, stock, tomato paste and sugar and pour into pan with prawn mixture. Bring to the boil, then reduce heat and simmer, uncovered, for 10 minutes.
3   Add basil and parsley. Cook for 2-3 minutes. Spoon sauce over hot, cooked pasta. Garnish with oysters in their shells.

❖

## COATED CHILLI RICE BALLS

Makes 16

- ☐ 3  teaspoons olive oil
- ☐ 1 onion, finely chopped
- ☐ 315 g (10 oz) long grain rice
- ☐ 1/2 teaspoon ground turmeric
- ☐ 750 mL (1 1/4 pt) chicken stock
- ☐ 1/2 teaspoon chilli powder
- ☐ freshly ground black pepper
- ☐ 3 spring onions (shallots), finely chopped

- ☐ 15 g (1/2 oz) butter
- ☐ 3 tablespoons grated tasty cheese
- ☐ 2 eggs, lightly beaten
- ☐ 125 g (4 oz) mozzarella cheese, cut into 1 cm (1/2 in) cubes
- ☐ 90 g (3 oz) dried breadcrumbs
- ☐ oil for cooking

1   Heat oil in a frypan and cook onion for 2-3 minutes or until tender. Stir in rice and turmeric and cook for 1-2 minutes or until rice is coated with oil.
2   Pour in 185 mL (6 fl oz) stock and bring to the boil. Cook, stirring frequently until liquid has almost evaporated. Add remaining stock, chilli powder and pepper to taste. Simmer for 10-15 minutes or until liquid has been absorbed. Remove pan from heat and stir through spring onions, butter and tasty cheese.
3   Lightly fold eggs through, taking care not to mash rice grains. Divide rice mixture into sixteen equal portions. Take a cheese cube and with hands, mould one portion of rice around cheese, to form a ball. Repeat with remaining rice and cheese portions.
4   Coat balls in breadcrumbs and refrigerate for 30 minutes. Heat oil in a deep saucepan and cook four to five balls at a time, until golden. Remove, drain on absorbent kitchen paper and serve.

*Coated Chilli Rice Balls*

Bowls from Lifestyle Imports

## TUNA AND OLIVE SAUCE

Serves 4

- ☐ **30 g (1 oz) butter**
- ☐ **2 tablespoons plain flour**
- ☐ **125 mL (4 fl oz) milk**
- ☐ **3 tablespoons chicken stock**
- ☐ **425 g (14 oz) tuna in brine, drained and liquid reserved**
- ☐ **1 tablespoon finely chopped fresh dill**
- ☐ **12 black olives, pitted and sliced**
- ☐ **2 tablespoons capers, finely chopped**
- ☐ **2-3 drops Tabasco sauce**
- ☐ **3 tablespoons single cream**
- ☐ **2 tablespoons lemon juice**
- ☐ **freshly ground black pepper**

1  Melt butter in a saucepan, add flour and cook for 1 minute. Remove from heat.
2  Blend in milk, stock and tuna liquid, stirring over a medium heat until sauce boils and thickens.
3  Reduce heat and add dill, olives, capers, Tabasco, cream and lemon juice. Season to taste with pepper and stir well to combine.
4  Break up tuna into smaller chunks and fold through sauce. Cook for 2-3 minutes to heat through. Spoon sauce over hot, cooked pasta and serve.

## PASTA WITH MUSHROOM AND BACON SAUCE

*A rich creamy sauce that can be made in minutes. This sauce is best to use with the long varieties of pasta such as fettuccine.*

Serves 4

- ☐ **1 small head broccoli, cut into small florets**
- ☐ **2 teaspoons olive oil**
- ☐ **4 bacon rashers, chopped**
- ☐ **125 g (4 oz) button mushrooms, sliced**
- ☐ **1 clove garlic, crushed**
- ☐ **315 mL (10 fl oz) single cream**
- ☐ **freshly ground black pepper**
- ☐ **3 tablespoons finely chopped fresh parsley**

1  Boil, steam or microwave broccoli until just tender. Drain and refresh under cold running water. Drain and set aside.
2  Heat oil in a frypan and cook bacon for 3-4 minutes or until crisp. Stir in mushrooms and garlic and cook for 2-3 minutes.
3  Pour in cream, bring to the boil, stirring frequently and simmer for 5 minutes or until sauce thickens. Season to taste with pepper, add broccoli and heat through. Spoon sauce over hot, cooked pasta. Sprinkle with parsley and serve.

*Seafood and Tomato Sauce, Tuna and Olive Sauce, Pasta with Mushroom and Bacon Sauce*

### PASTA PERFECTION

The success to perfect pasta is in the cooking.

✧  For perfect results every time, allow approximately 4 litres (7 pt) of water to 500 g (1 lb) of pasta and use a very large saucepan. Bring the water to a rapid boil, add a dash of oil and a pinch of salt. The oil prevents the pasta sticking and the salt helps bring out the flavour. Add the pasta, give a stir and cook for the required time.

✧  Pasta is cooked when it is 'al dente' (to the tooth tender but some resistance to the bite). It should not be overcooked and mushy.

✧  Cooking time varies, depending on the type of pasta you are cooking. Commercially packaged dried pasta takes 10-12 minutes to cook, while fresh pasta takes 3-5 minutes. Once cooked, drain in a colander and rinse under cold water if the pasta is to be used as a cold dish. If it is to be served hot, stir through a little oil or melted butter to prevent the pasta sticking.

*Napkin Holders from Bibelot*

❖

## AUBERGINE AND RICE PIE

*A very tasty adaptation of the ever popular recipe, moussaka*

Serves 6

- ☐ **2 large aubergines (eggplants), cut into $^1/_2$ cm ($^1/_4$ in) slices**
- ☐ **125 mL (4 fl oz) olive oil**
- ☐ **1 onion, chopped**
- ☐ **2 cloves garlic, crushed**
- ☐ **500 g (1 lb) lean minced beef**
- ☐ **425 g (14 oz) canned tomatoes, undrained and mashed**
- ☐ **1 tablespoon finely chopped fresh oregano**
- ☐ **2 tablespoons tomato paste**
- ☐ **freshly ground black pepper**
- ☐ **185 g (6 oz) brown rice, cooked**
- ☐ **250 g (8 oz) fresh or frozen peas, cooked**
- ☐ **90 g (3 oz) grated tasty cheese**
- ☐ **3 tablespoons grated Parmesan cheese**
- ☐ **4 tablespoons dried breadcrumbs**

*Aubergine and Rice Pie,
Cheesy Baked Rice Custard*

1  Brush aubergine with oil. Heat half the remaining oil in a frypan. Place a single layer of aubergine in pan and cook until golden on each side. Remove and drain on absorbent kitchen paper. Repeat with remaining aubergine.

2  Heat remaining oil in pan, cook onion and garlic for 2-3 minutes or until onion softens. Stir in meat and cook for 6-8 minutes, or until meat browns.

3  Combine tomatoes, oregano, tomato paste and pepper to taste. Pour into pan. Simmer for 8-10 minutes, or until liquid reduces by half. Remove pan from heat and add rice, peas, tasty and Parmesan cheeses.

4  Grease a 23 cm (9 in) deep, round cake pan. Sprinkle half the breadcrumbs over base and sides of pan. Place a layer of overlapping aubergine slices over base and sides of pan. Spoon meat mixture over aubergine. Pack down well using the back of a spoon.

5  Overlap remaining aubergine slices over filling. Sprinkle with remaining breadcrumbs. Bake at 180°C (350°F/Gas 4) for 25-30 minutes or until golden. Stand 5 minutes before turning out and serving.

### Just right rice

Wash rice before cooking, to remove any loose starch and prevent the grains sticking during cooking. Wash rice in a large sieve under cold running water, until the water running through the sieve is clear. Brown rice sometimes contains bits of husks; remove these by placing the rice in a bowl of water and any foreign bodies will float to the surface. There are several methods of cooking rice.

**Absorption method:** This is an easy way to cook rice, and the grains stay separate and fluffy. Brown and white rice can be cooked in this way. Bring 500 mL (16 fl oz) of water to boil in a heavy-based saucepan. Slowly add 220 g (7 oz) of rice and salt to taste and return to the boil. Stir once, cover, then reduce heat to as low as possible. Simmer gently; 20-25 minutes for white and quick-cooking brown rice, 50-55 minutes for brown rice. At the end of cooking time the rice should be tender and all the liquid absorbed. Remove cover. Fork lightly and allow the steam to escape for about 5 minutes, before serving. To cook larger quantities of rice by this method, increase liquid by 250 mL (8 fl oz) to every extra 220 g (7 oz) of rice.

**Rapid boil method:** Bring 2 litres ($3^1/_2$ pt) water to boil in a large saucepan and add salt to taste. Slowly add 220 g (7 oz) rice and boil rapidly; 12-15 minutes for white and quick-cooking brown rice and 30-40 minutes for brown, or until tender. Stir frequently during cooking.

**Steamed method:** Steaming is a popular Chinese method of cooking rice. Using this method the grains stay separate and fluffy. After washing 220 g (7 oz) rice, leave to drain and dry, then place in a heavy-based saucepan. Add enough water to cover the rice by 2.5 cm (1 in). Bring to the boil and boil rapidly until steam holes (tunnels) appear on the surface of the rice. Reduce heat to as low as possible. Cover with a tight fitting lid, or foil, and steam; 10 minutes for white and quick-cooking brown rice, and 25-30 minutes for brown, or until tender. Remove lid, fork lightly and stand 5 minutes before serving.

**Microwave method:** Place 220 g (7 oz) washed rice in a large, deep microwave-safe bowl. Add 375 mL (12 fl oz) boiling water. Cover with lid or plastic food wrap and cook on HIGH (100%) for 10-13 minutes for white and quick-cooking brown rice. Stir once during cooking. Stand covered for 5 minutes before serving. If cooking brown rice, increase the quantity of water to 750 mL (24 fl oz) and allow 30 minutes for cooking.

## LASAGNE

Serves 6

- ☐ **9 sheets instant lasagne pasta**
- ☐ **60 g (2 oz) grated tasty cheese**
- ☐ **2 tablespoons grated Parmesan cheese**

MEAT SAUCE
- ☐ **2 teaspoons olive oil**
- ☐ **1 onion, chopped**
- ☐ **2 cloves garlic, crushed**
- ☐ **2 bacon rashers, chopped**
- ☐ **125 g (4 oz) button mushrooms, sliced**
- ☐ **500 g (1 lb) lean minced beef**
- ☐ **425 g (14 oz) canned tomatoes, undrained and mashed**
- ☐ **125 mL (4 fl oz) red wine**
- ☐ **1/2 teaspoon dried basil**
- ☐ **1/2 teaspoon dried oregano**
- ☐ **1 teaspoon sugar**

SPINACH CHEESE SAUCE
- ☐ **30 g (1 oz) butter**
- ☐ **2 tablespoons plain flour**
- ☐ **250 mL (8 fl oz) milk**
- ☐ **125 mL (4 fl oz) single cream**
- ☐ **60 g (2 oz) grated tasty cheese**
- ☐ **250 g (8 oz) frozen spinach, thawed and drained**
- ☐ **freshly ground black pepper**

1   To make meat sauce, heat oil in a frypan and cook onion, garlic, bacon and mushrooms for 2-3 minutes, or until onion softens.

2   Add mince to pan and cook for 4-5 minutes, or until meat browns. Combine tomatoes, wine, basil, oregano and sugar and pour into pan. Bring to the boil, reduce heat, cover and simmer for 35 minutes, or until sauce thickens.

3   To make sauce, melt butter in a saucepan, add flour and cook for 1-2 minutes. Remove pan from heat and stir in milk and cream. Cook, stirring continuously, until sauce boils and thickens.

4   Remove pan from heat and stir in cheese and spinach. Season with pepper.

5   To assemble lasagne, spread one-third of cheese sauce over base of a lightly greased 28 x 18 cm (11 x 7 in) shallow ovenproof dish. Top with three lasagne sheets, spread half the meat sauce over, then another third of spinach cheese sauce. Top with another three lasagne sheets and remaining meat sauce. Place remaining lasagne sheets over meat sauce and top with remaining cheese sauce.

6   Combine tasty and Parmesan cheeses and sprinkle over lasagne. Bake at 190°C (375°F/Gas 5) for 40 minutes or until golden.

## CHEESY BAKED RICE CUSTARD

*A baked rice custard with a difference – it has a surprise savoury flavour rather than sweet.*

Serves 4

- ☐ **30 g (1 oz) butter**
- ☐ **2 leeks, washed and sliced**
- ☐ **3 bacon rashers, chopped**
- ☐ **1/2 red pepper, finely chopped**
- ☐ **60 g (2 oz) short-grain rice, cooked**
- ☐ **375 mL (12 fl oz) milk**
- ☐ **2 eggs, lightly beaten**
- ☐ **1/2 teaspoon dry mustard**
- ☐ **1 teaspoon Worcestershire sauce**
- ☐ **1 tablespoon mayonnaise**
- ☐ **125 g (4 oz) grated tasty cheese**
- ☐ **2 tablespoons finely chopped fresh parsley**
- ☐ **1 teaspoon paprika**

1   Melt butter in a frypan. Cook leeks, bacon and pepper for 4-5 minutes, or until leeks soften and bacon browns. Remove pan from heat and stir rice through. Transfer rice mixture to an ovenproof dish.

2   Place milk in a saucepan and bring almost to the boil. Remove pan from heat and whisk in eggs, mustard, Worcestershire sauce, mayonnaise, cheese and parsley. Pour milk mixture over rice mixture. Sprinkle lightly with paprika.

3   Place ovenproof dish in a baking pan. Fill baking pan with hot water, so it comes halfway up the side of the ovenproof dish. Bake at 180°C (350°F/Gas 4) for 25-30 minutes, or until firm.

### COOK'S TIPS

✧ If you are using fresh pasta, separate the strands before cooking. When the water returns to the boil, start the cooking time, maintaining a slow rolling boil. Stir just enough to separate the strands, or the pasta will release an excess of starch.

✧ As a simple guideline, allow 100 g (3 1/2 oz) per person of dried pasta for a main meal, or 60-75 g (2-2 1/2 oz) for an entree. Allow 155 g (5 oz) of fresh pasta for main meals and 75-100 g (2 1/2-3 1/2 oz) for entrées.

*Lasagne*

# Christmas dinner for ten

To make Christmas a celebration for all – including the cook – to enjoy, follow the valuable advice below on everything from planning, to making the cake, the pudding and cooking the turkey.

## STUFFED TURKEY FILLETS

*We have chosen a boneless turkey breast fillet, but you might like to use the traditional whole turkey. You can mix and match the stuffings and sauces to suit your taste. The stuffings are suitable to use with pork, turkey, duck or chicken.*

Serves 10

- ☐ **2 x 1 kg (2 lb) boneless turkey breast fillets**
- ☐ **125 mL (4 fl oz) water**
- ☐ **2 tablespoons polyunsaturated oil**

1   Lay turkey breasts out flat, skin side down on a large board. Using a sharp knife, cut the breasts horizontally, almost all the way through the centre. Open out breasts and place between two sheets of plastic food wrap. Pound lightly with a rolling pin to flatten slightly.
2   Place stuffing of your choice down the centre of fillet. Roll up to enclose stuffing and secure with toothpicks or tie with string at even intervals.
3   Place on a roasting rack in a baking dish. Pour water into the baking dish and brush turkey with oil. Cover and bake at 180°C (350°F/Gas 4) for 1¼ hours or until tender and cooked through. Stand covered for 15 minutes before slicing. Serve with sauce of your choice.

---

### STUFFINGS

✧  Any one of these stuffings can be used as described above or used to season a whole turkey.
✧  Stuffings can also be cooked separately. You might like to make and serve two or three stuffings.

---

## PESTO STUFFING

- ☐ **185 g (6 oz) fresh white breadcrumbs**
- ☐ **90 g (3 oz) butter, melted**
- ☐ **1 egg, lightly beaten**
- ☐ **3 cloves garlic, crushed**
- ☐ **60 g (2 oz) grated Parmesan cheese**
- ☐ **2 tablespoons finely chopped fresh basil**
- ☐ **60 g (2 oz) pine nuts, toasted**

Place breadcrumbs, butter, egg, garlic, Parmesan cheese, basil and pine nuts in a bowl. Mix well to combine all ingredients.

## RAISIN, APPLE AND GINGER STUFFING

- ☐ **185 g (6 oz) fresh white breadcrumbs**
- ☐ **90 g (3 oz) butter, melted**
- ☐ **1 egg, lightly beaten**
- ☐ **30 g (1 oz) dried apple, roughly chopped**
- ☐ **3 tablespoons raisins, chopped**
- ☐ **2 tablespoons grated fresh root ginger**
- ☐ **2 tablespoons honey**
- ☐ **¼ teaspoon ground cinnamon**
- ☐ **125 g (4 oz) minced pork**

Place breadcrumbs, butter, egg, apple, raisins, ginger, honey, cinnamon and pork in a bowl and mix well to combine.

*Christmas Pudding with Hard Butter Sauce, Fruit Mince Tarts, Stuffed Turkey Fillets, Ginger and LIme Sauce, Ham with Apple and Citrus Glaze, Spicy Syrup Christmas Cake*

*China from Villeroy and Boch*

## FIG AND PECAN STUFFING

- ☐ **2 teaspoons oil**
- ☐ **1 large onion, chopped**
- ☐ **185 g (6 oz) soft white breadcrumbs**
- ☐ **90 g (3 oz) butter, melted**
- ☐ **1 egg, lightly beaten**
- ☐ **2 sticks celery, finely sliced**
- ☐ **155 g (5 oz) chopped dried figs**
- ☐ **90 g (3 oz) pecan nuts, chopped**
- ☐ **2 tablespoons finely chopped fresh parsley**
- ☐ **2 teaspoons ground cardamom**
- ☐ **3 teaspoons ground coriander**
- ☐ **2 teaspoons ground ginger**
- ☐ **freshly ground black pepper**

1   Heat oil in a frypan and cook onion for 4-5 minutes or until golden.
2   Place breadcrumbs, butter, egg, onion, celery, figs, pecans, parsley, cardamom, coriander, ginger and pepper in a bowl and mix well to combine.

## TOMATO SAUCE

- ☐ **1 red pepper, quartered**
- ☐ **2 tomatoes, peeled, seeded and chopped**
- ☐ **30 g (1 oz) butter**
- ☐ **1 onion, finely chopped**
- ☐ **6 peppercorns**
- ☐ **1 small bay leaf**
- ☐ **1¹/₂ tablespoons tomato paste**
- ☐ **125 mL (4 fl oz) chicken stock**

1   Grill pepper until skin blisters and blackens. Allow to cool, then peel off skin.
2   Place pepper and tomatoes into a food processor or blender and process until smooth.
3   Melt butter in a frypan and cook onion for 2-3 minutes or until soft. Stir in tomato mixture, peppercorns, bay leaf, tomato paste and chicken stock. Simmer for 20 minutes, or until sauce reduces and thickens.

## GINGER AND LIME SAUCE

- ☐ **15 g (¹/₂ oz) butter**
- ☐ **3 cloves garlic, finely sliced**
- ☐ **2 teaspoons grated fresh ginger**
- ☐ **375 mL (12 fl oz) stock, made from strained pan juices and chicken stock**
- ☐ **4 tablespoons lime marmalade**
- ☐ **125 mL (4 fl oz) Madeira**
- ☐ **1¹/₂ tablespoons cornflour blended with 3 tablespoons water**

1   Melt butter in a saucepan and cook garlic and ginger for 1-2 minutes. Stir in stock and cook over medium heat until mixture boils. Reduce heat and simmer for 10 minutes.
2   Strain mixture to remove garlic and ginger, then return to pan. Add lime marmalade and cornflour mixture and cook over a medium heat, stirring frequently until sauce boils and thickens.

## GRAVY MADE USING PAN JUICES

- ☐ **1¹/₂ tablespoons plain flour**
- ☐ **375 mL (12 fl oz) chicken stock**
- ☐ **1 teaspoon Worcestershire sauce**

1   Drain all but 2 tablespoons of juices from the baking pan. Place baking pan over heat, stir in flour and cook over a medium heat until lightly browned.
2   Remove pan from heat and gradually blend in stock and Worcestershire sauce. Return to heat and cook, stirring constantly until gravy boils and thickens. Strain gravy into a small saucepan and cover to prevent a skin forming. Reheat when required.

## RUM AND FRUIT GLAZE

- ☐ **60 g (2 oz) dried apricots**
- ☐ **60 g (2 oz) dried apples**
- ☐ **60 g (2 oz) raisins**
- ☐ **5 tablespoons freshly squeezed orange juice**
- ☐ **4 tablespoons dark rum**
- ☐ **185 g (6 oz) apricot jam, warmed and strained**
- ☐ **2 tablespoons brown sugar**
- ☐ **2 teaspoons dry mustard**
- ☐ **2 tablespoons golden syrup**
- ☐ **60 g (2 oz) morello cherries**
- ☐ **60 g (2 oz) seedless green grapes**
- ☐ **2 kiwi fruit, peeled and cut into 1 cm (¹/₂ in) cubes**
- ☐ **60 g (2 oz) pecan nuts**

1   Place apricots, apples and raisins in a bowl and pour over orange juice and rum. Cover and set aside to macerate for one hour, or preferably overnight.
2   Combine apricot jam, brown sugar, mustard and golden syrup. Spread half the mixture over the prepared ham. Drain dried fruit and arrange decoratively with cherries, grapes, kiwi fruit and pecans on top. Spoon over remaining glaze.

### Glazing and Storing the Ham

A glazed ham makes a delicious and stunning centrepiece for your Christmas table. These glazes will have your guests gasping in admiration at your talents. You can use either of the following glazes for cooked ham on the bone or canned ham.

**Ham on the bone:** Remove the rind, using a sharp knife to ease it away from the fat layer. Trim fat, leaving a thin layer. Score the surface of the fat in a diamond pattern, using the point of a sharp knife. Cut just through the surface; do not cut the fat too deeply or it will spread apart during cooking. Prepare the glaze and spread half, thinly, over the ham. Decorate with fruit and spoon over remaining glaze, taking care not to disturb the fruit arrangement. Place the ham into a lightly greased baking pan and bake at 180°C (350°F/Gas 4) for 1-1¹/₂ hours. Remove from oven and set aside to cool. Cover loosely with foil and store in the refrigerator until required.

**Canned ham:** Open the can at both ends, push ham out into a baking pan. Bake at 180°C (350°F/Gas 4) for 5-10 minutes or until jelly melts. Drain jelly from pan, brush ham with glaze and decorate with fruit as for ham on the bone. Bake at 180°C (350°F/Gas 4) for 15-20 minutes.

**Storing ham on the bone:** After your Christmas dinner, you usually find yourself left with an abundance of ham. Leftover ham will keep for up to four weeks if stored correctly. Wrap the ham loosely in a clean wet tea towel or pillowcase and store in the refrigerator. Rinse and wring out the tea towel or pillowcase daily and replace around ham. Do not store ham in plastic or the original cheesecloth in which it was packaged.

## APPLE AND CITRUS GLAZE

- ☐ **185 g (6 oz) apricot jam, warmed and strained**
- ☐ **2 tablespoons demerara sugar**
- ☐ **2 teaspoons honey**
- ☐ **2 green apples, peeled, cored, halved and thinly sliced**
- ☐ **2 oranges, peeled and thinly sliced**

Combine jam, sugar and honey; spread half the mixture over prepared ham. Arrange alternate slices of apple and orange on top, then spoon remaining glaze over.

## ❖
## BASIC FRUIT MIXTURE

*This basic fruit mixture is designed for those who wish to to make the most of their time during the Christmas season. Make the mixture up to one month in advance and store it in an airtight container, in the refrigerator. Stir the fruit occasionally. In this recipe Midori liqueur (melon liqueur) has been used but you may like to use brandy or sweet sherry instead. This amount of mixture is sufficient to make a Christmas cake, a pudding and twenty-four mince tarts.*

- [ ] 1 kg (2 lb) sultanas, halved
- [ ] 375 g (12 oz) currants
- [ ] 170 g (5¹/₂ oz) raisins, chopped
- [ ] 30 g (1 oz) mixed peel, chopped
- [ ] 155 g (5 oz) pitted dried dates, chopped into small pieces
- [ ] 170 g (5¹/₂ oz) dried apricots, chopped into small pieces
- [ ] 155 g (5 oz) pitted prunes, chopped into small pieces
- [ ] 250 g (8 oz) glacé cherries, quartered
- [ ] 155 g (5 oz) glacé pineapple, chopped into small pieces
- [ ] 75 g (2¹/₂ oz) angelica, chopped
- [ ] ¹/₂ honeydew melon, peeled, seeded and chopped
- [ ] 375 g (12 oz) golden syrup
- [ ] 250 mL (8 fl oz) Midori liqueur

Place sultanas, currants, raisins, mixed peel, dates, apricots, prunes, cherries, pineapple, honeydew and angelica in a large mixing bowl. Stir in golden syrup and liqueur; mix well to combine. Cover tightly with plastic food wrap and stand overnight, or transfer to an airtight container and store in the refrigerator until required.

*Making a boiled Christmas Pudding*

## CHRISTMAS PUDDING

*You can either steam or boil this pudding, choose whichever method you prefer.*

Serves 8

- [ ] **250 g (8 oz) butter, softened**
- [ ] **60 g (2 oz) couscous**
- [ ] **3 eggs, lightly beaten**
- [ ] **4 tablespoons golden syrup**
- [ ] **125 g (4 oz) soft rye breadcrumbs**
- [ ] **220 g (7 oz) ground hazelnuts**
- [ ] **$^1/_4$ quantity Basic Fruit Mixture**

Cream butter until pale and creamy. Add couscous, eggs and golden syrup and beat well. Fold in breadcrumbs, ground hazelnuts and the fruit mixture. Steam or boil pudding for $2^1/_2$ hours for small puddings or 4 hours for large puddings.

## SPICY SYRUP CHRISTMAS CAKE

Makes 1 cake

- [ ] **250 g (8 oz) butter**
- [ ] **410 g (13 oz) semolina**
- [ ] **5 eggs, lightly beaten**
- [ ] **220 g (7 oz) caster sugar**
- [ ] **2 teaspoons mixed spice**
- [ ] **1 teaspoon grated orange peel**
- [ ] **$^1/_2$ quantity Basic Fruit Mixture**

SYRUP
- [ ] **1 orange**
- [ ] **375 mL (12 fl oz) water**
- [ ] **375 g (12 oz) sugar**
- [ ] **1 cinnamon stick**

1   Place butter in a large mixing bowl and beat until light and creamy. Add semolina and beat in eggs one at a time, beating well after each addition.
2   Add caster sugar a little at a time, beating well after each addition. Stir in spice, orange peel and fruit mixture. Mix well to combine. Spoon mixture into a 23 cm (9 in) lined, square cake tin. Bake at 160°C (325°F/Gas 3) for $2^1/_2$-3 hours or until cooked.
3   To make syrup, cut two to three thin strips of peel only, from the orange, using a vegetable peeler. Place water, sugar, cinnamon stick and orange peel in a saucepan and cook over medium heat, stirring constantly until sugar dissolves. Bring syrup to the boil without stirring, then reduce heat and simmer for 10 minutes. Set aside to cool slightly, then strain.
4   Remove cake from oven. Pour syrup over and set aside to cool in cake tin.

---

### PREPARING THE CAKE PAN

To achieve good, evenly shaped Christmas cakes, line your cake tin with heavy duty aluminium foil, placing the shiny side against the tin and dull side against the cake. Cut three strips of newspaper or brown paper 2.5 cm (1 in) wider than sides of the cake tin. Position these strips around the tin and secure with string. The newspaper acts as an insulator and prevents the outside of the cake burning.

---

## FRUIT MINCE TARTS

Makes 24

FILLING
- [ ] **2 tablespoons golden syrup**
- [ ] **125 g butter (4 oz), frozen and grated**
- [ ] **$^1/_4$ quantity Basic Fruit Mixture**

ALMOND PASTRY
- [ ] **250 g (8 oz) plain flour**
- [ ] **125 g (4 oz) butter, chilled and cut into small pieces**
- [ ] **170 g ($5^1/_2$ oz) caster sugar**
- [ ] **60 g (2 oz) ground almonds**
- [ ] **3 drops almond essence**
- [ ] **4-5 tablespoons iced water**
- [ ] **icing sugar for dusting**

1   To make filling, place golden syrup, butter and fruit mixture in a mixing bowl. Mix lightly to combine and set aside.
2   To make pastry, sift flour into a large mixing bowl. Rub through butter with fingertips, until mixture resembles fine breadcrumbs. Stir in sugar, almonds, essence and enough water to mix to a firm dough. Refrigerate for 30 minutes. Roll out pastry to 5 mm ($^1/_4$ in) in thickness. Cut pastry into twenty-four 7.5 cm (3 in) rounds and twenty-four 5 cm (2 in) rounds, using metal pastry cutters. Place larger pastry rounds in lightly greased patty tins. Spoon in filling and top with smaller pastry rounds. Press edges together and bake at 180°C (350°F/Gas 4) for 15-20 minutes or until pastry is golden and crisp. Stand in tins for 10 minutes before removing to a wire rack to cool. Serve warm, or at room temperature, dusted lightly with icing sugar.

---

### IS YOUR CAKE COOKED?

Push a fine skewer into the centre of your cake. When cooked, the skewer will come out clean. If there are any traces of mixture on the skewer, cook for 20 minutes longer.

---

## HARD BUTTER SAUCE

*Make the basic recipe or try one of the variations. Hard Butter Sauce can be made up to 3 months in advance and freeze it or store it in the refrigerator for up to a week.*

Makes 185 g (6 oz)

- [ ] **125 g (4 oz) butter, softened**
- [ ] **345 g (11 oz) icing sugar, sifted**

Beat butter until pale and creamy. Add icing sugar a little at a time, beating well after each addition until light and fluffy.

## PECAN AND LIQUEUR BUTTER SAUCE

- [ ] **1 quantity Hard Butter Sauce**
- [ ] **2 tablespoons Baileys Irish Cream**
- [ ] **3 tablespoons ground pecan nuts**

1   Make up Hard Butter Sauce as above and fold through Irish Cream and nuts.
2   Spoon mixture into a piping bag fitted with a large star piping nozzle. Pipe rosettes onto an oven tray, covered with aluminium foil and freeze until required. Remove from freezer 30 minutes prior to serving.

## BRANDIED ORANGE BUTTER SAUCE

- [ ] **1 quantity Hard Butter Sauce**
- [ ] **$1^1/_2$ tablespoons brandy**
- [ ] **2 teaspoons grated orange peel**

1   Make up Hard Butter Sauce as for the basic recipe, then fold through brandy and orange peel.
2   Spoon mixture onto a large piece of aluminium foil. Form into a rectangular shape with a spatula. Enclose with foil and freeze until required. Remove from freezer 30 minutes prior to serving and cut into slices to serve.

## ALMOND LIQUEUR BUTTER SAUCE

- [ ] **1 quantity Hard Butter Sauce**
- [ ] **2 tablespoons Amaretto**

1   Make up Hard Butter Sauce as for the basic recipe, then fold through Amaretto.
2   Spoon mixture onto a large piece of aluminium foil. Form into a rectangular shape with a spatula. Enclose with foil and freeze until required. Remove from freezer 30 minutes prior to serving and cut into slices to serve.

## Cooking the Pudding

**Boiling the pudding:** First prepare the pudding cloth. Purchase half a metre of unbleached calico, cut in half and trim to give two square pudding cloths. Soak calico overnight in cold water, then boil for 20 minutes and rinse well. Dip the prepared cloth into boiling water and, using rubber gloves to protect hands, wring excess water from cloth. Spread cloth out over a work surface and sprinkle with 5 tablespoons plain flour. Working quickly, rub flour into cloth, covering an area of about 38 cm (15 in) in diameter. The flour should be thicker in the centre of cloth. Spoon mixture into the centre of the cloth, then gather up the ends of cloth firmly around the pudding. Mould pudding with hands to form a smooth round shape. Tie with string as close to pudding as possible. Make a loop in the string for ease in lifting the pudding in and out of water and for hanging it after cooking. To ensure that the pudding is as round as possible pull the ends of the cloth tightly. Three-quarters fill a large saucepan with water and bring to the boil. Quickly, but gently, lower the pudding into the water, cover and boil rapidly for the required time. Add more boiling water as it evaporates. There must be enough water in the boiler at all times for the pudding to move freely and float. When the cooking is complete, remove pudding from saucepan using the handle of a wooden spoon placed through the string handle. Carefully lift out of the water. Suspend the pudding from a drawer or cupboard handle. It is important for the pudding to be able to swing freely without touching anything. Keep cloth ends away from pudding by twisting them around the supporting string. The cloth will start to dry out in patches within a few minutes. Allow the pudding to dry overnight or until completely cold, then take it down. Cut the string and loosen cloth from top of pudding. Remove any excess flour. Set aside at room temperature until top of cloth is completely dry – this could take a day or two. Retie pudding cloth and store pudding in an airtight container in the refrigerator until required. Remove the pudding from the refrigerator about twelve hours before it is to be reheated. Boil the pudding for 1 hour and then suspend as before for 10 minutes. Cut the string and carefully remove the cloth to expose one-quarter of the pudding. Using a towel to protect your hands invert the pudding onto a serving plate, then slowly and carefully pull away the cloth. Leave the pudding to stand at room temperature for 20 minutes before cutting. The longer the pudding stands the darker the skin will become.

**Steaming the pudding:** Spoon the pudding mixture into a well-greased china or aluminium pudding basin. Cover with a large piece of greased aluminium foil. If basin has a lid, place the lid over the foil and bring surplus foil up over it. If the basin has no lid, tie the foil securely in position, using string. Lower pudding into a large saucepan containing sufficient boiling water to come halfway up the side of the basin. Add more boiling water as required during cooking. On completion of cooking remove and set aside to cool to room temperature. Refrigerate in basin for up to six weeks. On the day of serving steam for 1 hour then turn out and serve.

*Spicy Syrup Christmas Cake*

# Chocolate making

Chocolate making is easy and lots of fun. It is an inexpensive way to make personalised gifts for your special friends or family. As with most skills, practice makes perfect.

## Melting chocolate

✧ Chocolate melts more rapidly if broken into small pieces.

✧ The melting process should occur slowly, as chocolate scorches if overheated.

✧ To melt chocolate, place it in the top of saucepan and set aside. Fill the bottom part of saucepan with enough water to come just under top pan, the water should not touch the top pan. Bring water to the boil, then remove from heat and place chocolate over the hot water. Stand off the heat, stirring occasionally until chocolate melts and is of a smooth consistency. Cool at room temperature.

✧ Chocolate can be melted quickly and easily in the microwave. Place chocolate in a microwave-safe dish and cook on HIGH (100%) for 2 minutes per 410 g (13 oz) chocolate. When melting chocolate in the microwave you will find that it tends to hold its shape, so always stir it before additional heating. If the chocolate is not completely melted, cook it for an extra 30 seconds, then stir again.

## Storing chocolate

Chocolate should be stored in a dry, airy place at a temperature of about 16°C (60°F). If stored in unsuitable conditions, the cocoa butter in chocolate may rise to the surface, leaving a white film. A similar discoloration occurs when water condenses on the surface. This often happens to refrigerated chocolates that are too loosely wrapped. Chocolate affected this way is still suitable for melting, but not for grating.

## Moulded chocolates

**Solid chocolates:** It is important to have the moulds clean and dry. Fill the mould with melted chocolate and tap on a hard surface to remove any air bubbles. Place mould in the freezer for 3 minutes or until set. When set remove from freezer and tap mould gently to remove chocolates.

**Filled chocolates:** Quarter fill the mould with melted chocolate and tap to remove any air bubbles. Brush the chocolate evenly up the sides of the mould to make a shell and freeze 2 minutes or until set. Add a filling such as fondant, fruit or liqueur. Fill the top with melted chocolate and tap to remove air bubbles. Return mould to the freezer for 3 minutes or until set. Remove from freezer and tap gently to remove. Larger chocolate cases to hold desserts can also be made in this way, using foil-lined individual metal flan tins, brioche or muffin tins as the moulds. When set, remove from tins and fill with a dessert filling such as mousse or a flavoured cream.

**Marbled chocolates:** Spoon a little melted, white and dark chocolate separately into a dish. Using a teaspoon, swirl the white chocolate into the dark chocolate to make a marble pattern, then proceed as above.

---

### CHOCOLATE SUBSTITUTES

Compound chocolate, also called chocolate coating, is designed to replace couverture chocolate for coating. It can be purchased in block form or as round discs. Both forms are available in milk or dark chocolate. Compound chocolate is made from a vegetable oil base with sugar, milk solids and flavouring. It contains cocoa powder, but not cocoa butter and is easy to melt; it does not require tempering and is the easiest form for beginners to work with.

## *Chocolate Decorations*

**Chocolate caraques:** Pour melted chocolate over a cool work surface such as marble, ceramic or granite. Spread the chocolate as smoothly as possible using a flexible metal spatula, into a very thin layer; do not leave any holes. If the chocolate is too thick it will not roll. Allow chocolate to set at room temperature. Holding a long sharp knife at a 45° angle, pull gently over the surface of the chocolate to form curls.

**Chocolate curls and shavings:** Chocolate curls are made from chocolate that is at room temperature. To make shavings, chill the chocolate first. Using a vegetable peeler, shave the sides of the chocolate. Curls or shavings will fall depending on the temperature of the chocolate.

**Chocolate leaves:** Use stiff, fresh, non-poisonous leaves such as rose or lemon leaves. Keep as much stem as possible to hold onto. Wash and dry leaves, brush the shiny surface of the leaf with a thin layer of melted, cooled chocolate. Allow to set to room temperature then carefully peel away leaf.

**Piping chocolate:** Chocolate can be piped into fancy shapes for decorating desserts or cakes. Trace a simple design on a thin piece of paper. Tape a sheet of baking paper to the work surface and slide the drawing under the sheet of paper. Pipe over outline with melted chocolate. Allow to set at room temperature, then remove carefully with a metal spatula.

*Chocolate making is lots of fun*

# Take a scone dough

Who can resist the aroma of freshly baked scones? This section is filled with tempting recipes that will show you how versatile a scone dough can be.

❖
## BASIC SCONES

*For many people, being able to make a perfect batch of scones is the ultimate test of cooking skills.*

Makes 10

- ☐ **250 g (8 oz) self-raising flour**
- ☐ **1 teaspoon baking powder**
- ☐ **2 teaspoons sugar**
- ☐ **60 g (2 oz) butter, chopped**
- ☐ **1 egg, lightly beaten**
- ☐ **125 mL (4 fl oz) milk**

1  Sift flour and baking powder together into a mixing bowl, add sugar. Rub in butter, using the fingertips, until mixture resembles fine breadcrumbs.
2  Make a well in the centre of the flour. Using a round-ended knife, mix the egg and almost all the milk through the flour. Mix to a soft dough, adding remaining milk if necessary.
3  Turn onto a lightly floured surface and knead lightly with fingertips until smooth. Using heel of hand, press dough out to 2 cm ($^3/_4$ in) thickness. Cut scones out using a floured 5 cm (2 in) scone cutter; do not twist cutter, or scones will rise unevenly.
4  Arrange scones close together on a greased and lightly floured oven tray, or in a 20 cm (8 in) sandwich tin. Brush tops with a little milk and bake at 220°C (425°F/Gas 7) for 15-20 minutes or until scones are golden brown and sound hollow when tapped with your fingertips.

---

### PERFECT SCONES

◇  Work quickly and have all the equipment cool.
◇  If you wrap scones in a clean tea towel when cooked, they will be soft and light. If you leave scones on a cooling rack they form a hard shell.
◇  Use the basic scone recipe to make a quick and easy pizza base.
◇  You can freeze scones for up to 3 months in an airtight container or a sealed freezer bag.

---

❖
## HAZELNUT SPIRAL

Serves 10

- ☐ **1 quantity basic scone dough with 2 teaspoons mixed spice added to flour**
- ☐ **125 g (4 oz) hazelnut spread**
- ☐ **90 g (3 oz) chopped hazelnuts**

GLAZE
- ☐ **1 tablespoon water**
- ☐ **2 tablespoons sugar**
- ☐ **2 tablespoons honey**

1  Roll scone dough out, on a lightly floured surface, to form a rectangle 1 cm in thickness. Spread with hazelnut spread and sprinkle with hazelnuts. Roll up like a Swiss roll, starting from longer end. Using a sharp knife, cut slits three-quarters of the way through roll, 2.5 cm (1 in) apart.
2  Place roll on a lightly greased and floured oven tray and shape into a horseshoe. Twist each slice upwards so that the filling shows. Bake at 220°C (425°F/Gas 7) for 15-20 minutes, or until golden and sounds hollow when tapped.
3  To make glaze, place water, sugar and honey in a small saucepan and heat, stirring constantly, until sugar dissolves and ingredients are well combined. Bring to the boil and simmer for 2 minutes. Remove from heat and brush over warm Hazelnut Spiral.

*Glassware from HAG*

*Left: Basic Scones*
*Above Right: Pumpkin Damper, Apple Dumplings in Caramel Sauce, Pesto Pinwheels, Hazelnut Spiral*

## PUMPKIN DAMPER

Serves 8

- [ ] 250 g (8 oz) self-raising flour
- [ ] 1 teaspoon baking powder
- [ ] 1 teaspoon ground mixed spice
- [ ] 1 teaspoon ground nutmeg
- [ ] 2 teaspoons sugar
- [ ] 60 g (2 oz) butter, chopped
- [ ] 100 g (3$^1$/$_2$ oz) chopped prunes
- [ ] 250 g (8 oz) mashed pumpkin
- [ ] 4 tablespoons water

1  Sift flour, baking powder, mixed spice and nutmeg together in a bowl. Add sugar. Rub in butter, using the fingertips until mixture resembles fine breadcrumbs. Stir in prunes.

2  Make a well in the centre of the flour and, using a round-ended knife, mix in the pumpkin and water. Mix to a soft dough.

3  Turn onto a lightly floured surface and knead dough lightly until smooth. Shape into a round 18 cm (7 in) in diameter. Place on a greased and lightly floured baking tray. Brush top lightly with milk and sprinkle with a little extra flour. Mark into eight wedges, using a sharp knife and bake at 220°C (425°F/Gas 7) for 10 minutes. Reduce heat to 180°C (350°F/Gas 4) and cook for 50 minutes longer, or until cooked.

## PESTO PINWHEELS

Makes 10

- [ ] 1 quantity basic scone dough
- [ ] 2 tablespoons milk
- [ ] 60 g (2 oz) tasty grated cheese

PESTO FILLING
- [ ] 90 g (3 oz) loosely packed fresh basil leaves
- [ ] 3 cloves garlic, crushed
- [ ] 3 tablespoons pine nuts, toasted
- [ ] 3 tablespoons olive oil
- [ ] 3 tablespoons grated Parmesan cheese
- [ ] freshly ground black pepper

1  To make filling, place basil, garlic, pine nuts and 2 tablespoons of oil in a food processor and process until combined. With machine running, gradually add remaining oil. Transfer to a small bowl, mix in cheese and season with pepper.

3  Roll out scone dough, on a lightly floured surface, to form a rectangle 1 cm ($^1$/$_2$ in) in thickness. Spread with filling and roll up like a Swiss roll. Cut roll into 2 cm ($^3$/$_4$ in) wide slices. Place slices on a lightly greased and floured oven tray, brush each with a little milk and sprinkle with cheese. Bake at 220°C (425°F/Gas 5) for 15-20 minutes, or until cooked.

## APPLE DUMPLINGS IN CARAMEL SAUCE

Serves 8

- [ ] 1 quantity basic scone dough
- [ ] 2 apples, peeled, cored and each cut into eight wedges

CARAMEL SAUCE
- [ ] 345 g (11 oz) brown sugar
- [ ] 2 tablespoons golden syrup
- [ ] 2 cups water
- [ ] 60 g (2 oz) butter
- [ ] 1 teaspoon vanilla

1  Roll dough out to 5 mm ($^1$/$_4$ in) thickness and cut into rounds using a floured 9 cm (3$^1$/$_2$ in) scone cutter. Place an apple wedge on one half of each round, brush rim with a little milk, fold over and seal by pinching with fingertips.

2  To make sauce, place sugar, golden syrup, water, butter and vanilla in a saucepan and heat, stirring constantly, until sugar dissolves and butter melts. Bring to the boil and simmer for 2 minutes.

3  Transfer sauce to a casserole, drop dumplings in and cook at 180°C (350°F/Gas 4) for 35-40 minutes or until sauce thickens and dumplings are cooked through.

# Take a butter cake

Add interest to your cakes by cooking them in differently shaped tins. The following recipe works perfectly if you follow the cooking times given in the chart.

### ❖
### BASIC BUTTER CAKE

- ☐ **125 g (4 oz) butter**
- ☐ **1 teaspoon vanilla essence**
- ☐ **185 g (6 oz) caster sugar**
- ☐ **2 eggs**
- ☐ **185 g (6 oz) plain flour, sifted**
- ☐ **1 1/2 teaspoons baking powder**
- ☐ **125 mL (4 fl oz) milk**

1  Cream butter and vanilla in a small mixing bowl until light and fluffy. Add sugar gradually, beating well after each addition.
2  Beat in eggs one at a time. Combine flour and baking powder and fold in alternately with milk. Spoon mixture into prepared cake tin.
3  Bake according to size of cake tin you have chosen. Stand 5 minutes before turning out onto a wire rack to cool. When cool, ice with frosting of your choice.

### *Variations*

**Chocolate cake:** Mix 60 g (2 oz) melted chocolate into the basic cake mixture before adding flour and milk. Replace 2 tablespoons of flour with 2 tablespoons cocoa powder. Bake according to tin size. Stand 5 minutes before turning out.

**Apple cake:** Spread two-thirds of the cake mixture into the prepared cake tin. Top with 200 g (6 1/2 oz) stewed apple, then remaining cake mixture. Bake according to cake tin size. Stand 10 minutes before turning out.

**Orange cake:** Replace vanilla with 2 teaspoons grated orange peel when creaming butter. Substitute 4 tablespoons orange juice for milk. Bake according to cake tin size. Stand 5 minutes before turning out.

**Coffee cake:** Replace vanilla with 1 tablespoon instant coffee dissolved in 1 tablespoon boiling water. Cool then cream with butter. Bake according to cake tin size. Stand 5 minutes before turning out.

**Coconut cake:** Replace vanilla with 1/2 teaspoon coconut essence and add 45 g (1 1/2 oz) desiccated coconut with flour and baking powder. Bake according to cake tin size. Stand 5 minutes then turn out.

**Banana cake:** Omit milk and add 3 small very ripe mashed bananas to creamed butter and egg mixture. Combine flour, baking powder and 1 teaspoon bicarbonate of soda, and fold into butter and egg mixture. Bake according to cake tin size. Stand 5 minutes before turning out.

### ❖
### LEMON CREAM CHEESE FROSTING

- ☐ **125 g (4 oz) cream cheese**
- ☐ **1 teaspoon grated lemon peel**
- ☐ **250 g (8 oz) icing sugar, sifted**
- ☐ **2 teaspoons lemon juice**

Beat cream cheese in a small mixing bowl until creamy. Add lemon peel, icing sugar and lemon juice and mix well. Use as desired.

## CHOCOLATE FROSTING

- ☐ **90 g (3 oz) butter**
- ☐ **250 g (8 oz) icing sugar, sifted**
- ☐ **1 tablespoon cocoa powder, sifted**
- ☐ **2 tablespoons single cream**

Beat butter in a small bowl until creamy. Add icing sugar, cocoa powder and cream. Beat until frosting is a spreading consistency. Use as desired.

## ORANGE CREAM FROSTING

- ☐ **60 g (2 oz) cream cheese**
- ☐ **2 tablespoons single cream**
- ☐ **1 teaspoon grated orange peel**
- ☐ **250 g (8 oz) icing sugar, sifted**

Beat cream cheese, cream and orange peel in a small mixing bowl until creamy. Add icing sugar and beat until smooth. Use as desired.

## PREPARATION AND COOKING TIMES

| TIN SIZE PREPARATION | | TEMPERATURE | COOKING TIME |
|---|---|---|---|
| 20 cm (8 in) ring tin | Grease and line | 180°C (350°F/Gas 4) | 40 mins |
| 20 cm (8 in) deep round tin | Grease and line | 180°C (350°F/Gas 4) | 50 mins |
| 20 cm (8 in) baba tin | Lightly grease | 180°C (350°F/Gas 4) | 40 mins |
| 14 x 21 cm (5 x 8 in) loaf tin | Grease and line | 180°C (350°F/Gas 4) | 60 mins |
| two x 8 x 26 cm (3 x 10 in) bar tins | Grease and line | 180°C (350°F/Gas 4) | 35 mins |
| 24 patty tins | Paper patty cake cases | 200°C (400°F/Gas 6) | 15 mins |

*From left: Basic Butter Cake with Lemon Cream Cheese Frosting, Orange Variation with Orange Cream Frosting, Coffee Variation*

## BEST EVER CHOCOLATE CELEBRATION CAKE

*This easy gâteau is sure to impress. For added effect you might like to decorate the top with chocolate curls, caraques or chocolate leaves. See page 59, for how to make these.*

- ☐ **90 g (3 oz) cocoa powder, sifted**
- ☐ **375 mL (12 fl oz) boiling water**
- ☐ **185 g (6 oz) butter**
- ☐ **375 g (12 oz) caster sugar**
- ☐ **2 tablespoons cherry conserve**
- ☐ **3 eggs**
- ☐ **315 g (10 oz) self-raising flour, sifted**
- ☐ **100 g (3¹/2 oz) toasted flaked almonds, chopped**

### CHERRY FILLING
- ☐ **3 tablespoons cherry conserve**
- ☐ **100 g (3¹/2 oz) icing sugar**
- ☐ **3 tablespoons ground almonds**
- ☐ **2 teaspoons Kirsch**

### COFFEE FROSTING
- ☐ **60 g (2 oz) butter**
- ☐ **250 g (8 oz) icing sugar, sifted**
- ☐ **2 teaspoons instant coffee, dissolved in 1 tablespoon boiling water**

1   Combine cocoa powder and boiling water. Mix to dissolve. Set aside to cool completely.

2   Cream butter, sugar and jam until light and fluffy. Beat in eggs one at a time, adding a little flour with each egg. Fold in remaining flour and cocoa mixture, alternately.

3   Spoon mixture into two greased and lined 20 cm (8 in) shallow cake tins. Bake at 180°C (350°F/Gas 4) for 35 minutes, or until cooked when tested with a skewer. Cool in tin for 5 minutes before turning out onto a wire rack to cool completely.

4   To make filling, place conserve, icing sugar, almonds and Kirsch in a bowl. Mix well until combined.

5   To make frosting, beat butter in a small mixing bowl until creamy. Add icing sugar and cooled coffee mixture and beat until frosting is of spreading consistency. Place one cake layer on a serving plate and spread with filling. Top with remaining cake layer and spread frosting over top and sides of cake. Press almonds onto sides of cake and decorate top with chocolate caraques or leaves.

*Best Ever Chocolate Celebration Cake*

# Take a biscuit

A quick and easy biscuit recipe is always an asset. It's ideal for lunchboxes, after school treats, or teatime with unexpected guests.

Glass Cake Stands from HAG

## BASIC BISCUIT RECIPE

Makes 40

- ☐ **125 g (4 oz) butter**
- ☐ **1 teaspoon vanilla essence**
- ☐ **185 g (6 oz) caster sugar**
- ☐ **1 egg**
- ☐ **125 g (4 oz) plain flour, sifted**
- ☐ **125 g (4 oz) self-raising flour, sifted**

1  Cream butter, sugar and vanilla until light and fluffy. Add egg and beat well. Fold in plain and self-raising flours, cover and refrigerate for 2 hours.

2  Roll heaped teaspoonfuls of mixture into balls. Place onto a greased oven tray, spacing well apart to allow for spreading. Flatten each biscuit slightly with a fork and bake at 180°C (350°F/Gas 4) for 12-15 minutes or until golden brown. Allow to cool on tray for a few minutes then transfer to a wire rack to finish cooking.

### *Variations*

**Spicy Fruit Cookies:** Replace 4 tablespoons of the caster sugar with 4 tablespoons brown sugar. Sift 2 teaspoons of cinnamon, 1 teaspoon of mixed spice and 1 teaspoon of ginger with the flour. Roll out mixture and cut 16 rounds with a biscuit cutter. Place teaspoonfuls of fruit mince on half the rounds and cover with remaining rounds. Press the edges lightly to seal and bake at 180°C (350°F/Gas 4) for 20-25 minutes, or until golden brown.

**Three-Chocolate Cookies:** Add 45 g (1 1/2 oz) finely chopped dark chocolate, 45 g (1 1/2 oz) finely chopped milk chocolate and 45 g (1 1/2 oz) finely chopped white chocolate to the biscuit mixture after adding the egg. Place spoonfuls on a greased oven tray and bake at 180°C (350°F/Gas 4) for 12-15 minutes or until golden.

**Creamy Jam Drops:** Roll mixture into balls and flatten slightly. Make indents in the centre of each round and fill with a small amount of cream cheese and top with a teaspoon of blackberry jam, or a jam of your choice. Be careful not to fill the holes too much, or the jam will overflow during cooking. Bake at 180°C (350°F/Gas 4) for 12-15 minutes, or until golden.

*Basic Biscuits, Spicy Fruit Cookies, Three-Chocolate Cookies, Creamy Jam Drops, Date Wraps*

## DATE WRAPS

Makes 20

- ☐ **20 dried dates, pitted**
- ☐ **4 tablespoons brandy**
- ☐ **1 quantity Basic Biscuit Recipe**

1  Soak dates in brandy for 30 minutes, then drain.

2  Divide biscuit dough into 20 equal portions. Mould each portion around a date. Place on a greased oven tray and bake at 160°C (325°F/Gas 3) for 20-25 minutes, or until golden brown.

# Take some pastry

## RICH SHORTCRUST PASTRY

Makes a 23 cm (9 in) flan case

- ☐ **250 g (8 oz) plain flour, sifted**
- ☐ **185 g (6 oz) butter, chilled and cut into small cubes**
- ☐ **1 egg yolk, lightly beaten**
- ☐ **3-4 tablespoons water, chilled**

1  Place flour into a medium bowl and rub in butter with fingertips until the mixture resembles breadcrumbs.

2  Mix in egg yolk and enough water to form a soft dough with a metal spatula or round-ended knife.

3  Turn onto a lightly floured surface and knead gently until smooth. Wrap in plastic wrap and refrigerate for 30 minutes. Roll and use as desired.

---

## BAKING BLIND

✧  To bake blind means to precook the pastry case without the filling. This is done when the filling you are using requires little or no cooking.

✧  To bake blind, line the pastry case with greaseproof paper, a double layer of kitchen paper, or foil. Place uncooked rice or dried beans on the paper to weigh down the pastry, as this prevents it from rising during cooking. Make sure that you push the rice or beans right to the sides, to support them. Bake as directed.

---

*Butterscotch, Apple and Date Flan, Apple and Lemon Tartlets*

---

## BUTTERSCOTCH, APPLE AND DATE FLAN

Serves 8

### NUT PASTRY
- ☐ **60 g (2 oz) finely chopped hazelnuts**
- ☐ **1 teaspoon mixed spice**
- ☐ **ingredients for 1 quantity Rich Shortcrust Pastry**
- ☐ **vanilla essence**

### APPLE AND DATE FILLING
- ☐ **90 g (3 oz) butter**
- ☐ **4 cooking apples, peeled, cored and quartered**
- ☐ **100 g (3$^1$/$_2$ oz) fresh dates, chopped**
- ☐ **$^1$/$_2$ teaspoon cinnamon**
- ☐ **125 g (4 oz) brown sugar**
- ☐ **125 mL (4 fl oz) golden syrup**
- ☐ **125 mL (4 fl oz) water**
- ☐ **$^1$/$_2$ teaspoon vanilla essence**
- ☐ **60 g (2 oz) plain flour**
- ☐ **1 egg, lightly beaten**

1  To prepare pastry, combine hazelnuts and spice with flour and add a few drops vanilla essence to the egg yolk. Make as directed in basic recipe. Roll out pastry on a lightly floured surface and line a lightly greased 23 cm (9 in) deep flan tin. Rest in refrigerator for 15 minutes. Place on an oven tray and blind bake at 220°C (425°F/Gas 7) for 10 minutes. Remove beans and paper and cook for 10 minutes longer.

2  To make filling, cut each apple quarter into four slices. Melt 60 g (2 oz) butter in a frypan and cook apples for 3-4 minutes. Remove from pan and arrange over pastry case. Sprinkle with dates and cinnamon.

3  Place sugar, golden syrup, water, remaining butter and vanilla in a saucepan and cook over a medium heat until sugar has dissolved. Bring to the boil and simmer for 2 minutes.

4  Remove from heat and cool for 15 minutes. Beat in flour and egg. Pour over apples and bake at 180°C (350°F/Gas 4) for 40-45 minutes or until filling is set. Serve hot or cold.

---

## APPLE AND LEMON TARTLETS

Makes 24

### SWEET PASTRY CASES
- ☐ **3 tablespoons caster sugar**
- ☐ **vanilla essence**
- ☐ **ingredients for 1 quantity Rich Shortcrust Pastry**
- ☐ **3 tablespoons ground almonds**

## FILLING

- [ ] **4 cooking apples, peeled, cored and chopped**
- [ ] **2 tablespoons grated lemon peel**
- [ ] **3 tablespoons water**
- [ ] **1 teaspoon cinnamon**
- [ ] **5 tablespoons lemon juice**
- [ ] **250 g (8 oz) sugar**
- [ ] **4 eggs, lightly beaten**
- [ ] **125 g (4 oz) butter, chopped**

1   To prepare pastry cases, add sugar to flour and a few drops vanilla essence to egg yolk. Continue as directed in basic recipe. Roll out pastry on a lightly floured surface and sprinkle with ground almonds. Cut out rounds, using a 5 cm (2 in) pastry cutter, and place in greased patty tins. Prick bases with a fork and rest them in refrigerator for 15 minutes. Bake at 200°C (400°F/Gas 6) for 15-20 minutes or until golden brown. Remove from oven and cool on a wire rack.

2   To make filling, place apples, lemon peel, water and cinnamon in a saucepan, bring to the boil and simmer for 15-20 minutes, or until reduced to a pulp. Place in a food processor or blender and process until smooth.

3   Transfer apple mixture to the top of a double saucepan. Add lemon juice and sugar and heat gently, stirring constantly, until sugar dissolves.

4   Remove from heat, gradually stir in the eggs and then the butter. Return to a very low heat and cook, stirring constantly, until the mixture becomes thick and creamy. Remove from heat and set aside to cool. Shortly before serving, spoon filling into pastry cases.

❖

## CREAMY CHICKEN PIE

Serves 6

### CHEESE PASTRY

- [ ] **60 g (2 oz) grated tasty cheese**
- [ ] **1 teaspoon mustard powder**
- [ ] **$^1/_2$ teaspoon cayenne pepper**
- [ ] **ingredients for $^1/_2$ quantity Rich Shortcrust Pastry**

### CHICKEN FILLING

- [ ] **1 tablespoon olive oil**
- [ ] **750 g (1$^1/_2$ lb) chicken fillets, diced**
- [ ] **60 g (2 oz) butter**
- [ ] **1 clove garlic, crushed**
- [ ] **1 stick celery, chopped**
- [ ] **1 onion, chopped**
- [ ] **3 tablespoons plain flour**
- [ ] **250 mL (8 fl oz) chicken stock**
- [ ] **250 mL (8 fl oz) milk**
- [ ] **1 tablespoon chopped fresh parsley**

- [ ] **1 tablespoon chopped fresh rosemary**
- [ ] **freshly ground black pepper**

1   To prepare pastry, combine cheese, mustard and cayenne pepper and mix into flour. Continue as directed in basic recipe. Place in refrigerator to rest.

2   To make filling, heat oil in a large frypan and cook one-third of the chicken over a high heat for 3 minutes, or until cooked through. Remove from pan and repeat with remaining chicken.

3   Melt butter in frypan, add garlic, celery and onion and cook for 3-4 minutes, or until onion softens. Stir in flour and cook for 2 minutes longer. Remove pan from heat and stir in stock and milk. Return to heat, bring to the boil, stirring constantly, and simmer for 3 minutes. Add chicken, parsley and rosemary. Season to taste with pepper and set aside to cool.

4   Place filling into a pie dish. Roll out pastry to 5 mm ($^1/_4$ in) in thickness. Brush rim of pie dish with a little water and place the pastry over the filling. Trim edges with a knife and decorate as desired. Brush with a little milk and bake at 200°C (400°F/Gas 6) for 30-35 minutes or until golden.

### PASTRY-MAKING TIPS

✧ Place your utensils in the refrigerator to chill for 15-20 minutes before making pastry.

✧ The best pastry is made using chilled butter and water.

✧ Handle the pastry as little as possible.

✧ When you roll out the pastry roll away from you, lifting and turning to ensure an even thickness.

✧ Take care that you do not stretch the pastry when you are rolling it out.

✧ Rest the pastry in the refrigerator for 30 minutes before baking, this will minimise shrinkage during cooking.

✧ Cook pastry in a 220°C (425°F/ Gas 7) preheated oven.

✧ To make pastry in the food processor, place flour and butter in food processor and process to cut butter. Add egg yolk and water and process until dough is formed. Knead lightly and allow to rest before rolling.

*Creamy Chicken Pie*

# Take a custard

Custard is a favourite accompaniment to desserts and stewed fruits. It also forms the basis of many desserts.

## STIRRED CUSTARD

Makes 375 mL (12 fl oz)

- [ ] **185 mL (6 fl oz) milk, scalded**
- [ ] **1 tablespoon sugar**
- [ ] **3 eggs, lightly beaten**
- [ ] **185 mL (6 fl oz) single cream**
- [ ] **1/2 teaspoon vanilla**

1   Combine milk and sugar in a small saucepan and heat gently until sugar has dissolved.

2   Place eggs in top of a double saucepan. Gradually stir in milk, then cream. Heat over simmering water, stirring constantly, until custard evenly coats the back of a wooden spoon.

3   Remove from heat and place top section of saucepan in iced water to stop the cooking process. Stir in vanilla essence and use custard as desired.

## CREME ANGLAISE

*Crème Anglaise is a light custard sauce which is great served warm or chilled with fruit desserts and puddings.*

Makes 250 mL (8 fl oz)

- [ ] **3 egg yolks**
- [ ] **1 1/2 tablespoons sugar**
- [ ] **315 mL (10 fl oz) milk, scalded**
- [ ] **1/2 teaspoon vanilla essence**

1   Combine egg yolks and sugar in a bowl. Place over a saucepan of simmering water and beat until a ribbon trail forms.

2   Gradually add milk and vanilla, stirring constantly. Transfer to a heavy-based saucepan and cook custard over a low heat, stirring in a figure-eight pattern, until it thickens and coats the back of a wooden spoon. Do not allow the custard to boil.

3   Remove pan from heat and place in a bowl of ice. Stir until custard cools a little. Strain through a fine sieve if necessary.

### SOUFFLE-MAKING TIPS

✧ Make preparing the dish and heating the oven your first steps.

✧ A soufflé will rise more evenly if it is placed on an oven tray to cook.

✧ Stir in 2-3 spoonfuls of whisked egg whites first, then fold in the remaining whisked whites. This lightens the mixture and the whites are more easily accepted by it.

✧ The soufflé will collapse if you open the oven door during cooking.

## NUT BAVARIAN CREAM

*These creamy surprises are laced with a hazelnut praline; a delight to end any special meal. In this recipe the cream is served in chocolate cases, but if you wish they can be placed in small individual moulds.*

Serves 10

- ☐ **4 tablespoons water**
- ☐ **250 g (8 oz) sugar**
- ☐ **125 g (4 oz) hazelnuts, toasted**
- ☐ **250 mL (8 fl oz) single cream, whipped**
- ☐ **1 tablespoon gelatine, dissolved in 3 tablespoons boiling water and cooled**
- ☐ **1 quantity Crème Anglaise, cooled**
- ☐ **10 chocolate cases (page 59)**

1   Place water and sugar in a small saucepan and stir over a medium heat until sugar dissolves. Brush down sides of pan with a wet pastry brush. Bring to the boil and cook for 5-7 minutes, or until the toffee mixture turns golden brown.

2   Place hazelnuts on a greased oven slide and pour toffee over. When cool, place in a food processor or blender and process. Fold whipped cream through.

3   Stir gelatine mixture into Crème Anglaise. Chill over ice, stirring occasionally.

4   Fold the cream mixture through the Crème Anglaise as it begins to set. Spoon cream mixture into chocolate cases and refrigerate until set.

## INDIVIDUAL APRICOT TRIFLES

Serves 4

- ☐ **18 cm (7 in) sponge or butter cake, sliced**
- ☐ **125 g (4 oz) apricot jam**
- ☐ **425 g (14 oz) canned apricots, drained and sliced**
- ☐ **1 tablespoon ground nutmeg**
- ☐ **3 tablespoons apricot nectar**
- ☐ **3 tablespoons brandy**
- ☐ **1 quantity 375 mL (12 fl oz) stirred custard**

1   Spread cake with jam. Place half the cake in the base of four individual dishes, top with half the apricots and sprinkle with a little nutmeg. Repeat layers with remaining cake, apricots and nutmeg.

2   Divide apricot nectar, brandy and custard into four portions and pour over cake and apricots. Cover and refrigerate until ready to serve.

## LAYERED STRAWBERRY SOUFFLE

Serves 6

- ☐ **2 tablespoons Amaretto liqueur**
- ☐ **2 tablespoons Grand Marnier**
- ☐ **250 g (8 oz) strawberries, hulled and sliced**
- ☐ **4 egg yolks**
- ☐ **90 g (3 oz) caster sugar**
- ☐ **4 tablespoons flour**
- ☐ **315 mL (10 fl oz) milk, scalded**
- ☐ **1/2 teaspoon vanilla essence**
- ☐ **5 egg whites**

1   Combine Amaretto and Grand Marnier, add strawberries and set aside to macerate for 30 minutes.

2   Beat egg yolks and sugar until thick and light then fold in flour. Combine milk and vanilla and whisk into egg mixture.

3   Transfer to a saucepan and heat gently, stirring until sauce boils and thickens. Reduce heat and simmer for 2 minutes.

4   Whisk egg whites until stiff peaks form. Fold quickly and lightly through sauce, using a metal spoon. Place half the strawberries in the base of a lightly greased 20 cm (8 in) soufflé dish with collar attached and pour over half the soufflé mixture. Repeat with remaining fruit and mixture.

5   Cook at 180°C (350°F/Gas 4) for 25-30 minutes, or until well risen and golden.

---

### SOUFFLE COLLARS

To make a soufflé collar, cut a piece of greaseproof paper 5 cm (2 in) longer than the circumference of the soufflé dish. Fold in half lengthwise to give a double thickness. Brush with melted butter and sprinkle with dry breadcrumbs, for a savoury soufflé, or caster sugar for a sweet soufflé. Wrap the paper collar around the soufflé dish. The soufflé dish should also be greased and sprinkled with breadcrumbs or sugar; the collar should extend about 5 cm (2 in) above the rim of the dish. Tie in place with string.

---

*Left: Nut Bavarian Cream,*
*Individual Apricot Trifles*
*Above: Layered Strawberry Soufflé*

# Take some fruit

Fruit makes a wonderful dessert served on its own or try one of the delicious fruit desserts below.

## ❖ FRUIT PLATTER WITH CREAMY APRICOT SAUCE

Serves 4

- ☐ 155 g (5 oz) dried apricot halves
- ☐ 250 mL (8 fl oz) boiling water
- ☐ 375 g (12 oz) thick sour cream or unflavoured yogurt
- ☐ 2 tablespoons brown sugar
- ☐ 1 tablespoon dark rum
- ☐ selection of fruit, prepared and arranged on a platter

1 Soak apricots in water for 1 hour. Place in a food processor or blender and process until smooth.

2 Combine purée, sour cream, brown sugar and rum in a bowl and mix well. Serve with fruit as a dipping sauce.

### COOK'S TIP

Sauce may be made a day ahead and kept covered in the refrigerator.
❖ If you would like to serve the sauce hot, heat gently over a low heat in a small saucepan. Take care not to allow the sauce to boil.

### GELATINE TIPS

✧ To dissolve gelatine pour hot liquid into a container, sprinkle gelatine over and whisk with a fork until dissolved.
✧ The microwave is great for dissolving gelatine; mix the gelatine with cold water and cook on HIGH (100%) power for 45 seconds.
✧ In warm weather you may need to increase the gelatine quantity by half to ensure setting.
✧ Ensure that the gelatine mixture is the same temperature as the mixture to which it is to be added. If the two are at different temperatures tough strands form and separation occurs.

## ❖ INDIVIDUAL FRUIT POTS

*Quick and easy, these fruit jellies make a delicious dessert.*

Serves 6

- ☐ 155 g (5 oz) canned apricot halves
- ☐ 155 g (5 oz) strawberries, hulled and quartered
- ☐ 200 g (6 1/2 oz) black grapes
- ☐ 1 orange, segmented
- ☐ 2 tablespoons brandy
- ☐ 1 packet lemon jelly crystals
- ☐ 440 mL (14 fl oz) boiling water
- ☐ pulp 2 passion fruit

1 Soak apricots, strawberries, grapes and orange in brandy for 30 minutes.

2 Dissolve jelly crystals in water, set aside and allow to cool to room temperature. Stir in passion fruit.

3 Place half the fruit in six, wetted individual moulds. Cover with half the jelly, place in the refrigerator and allow to set. Top with remaining fruit and jelly and return to refrigerator until set.

## ❖ FRUIT CREPES WITH LEMON CREAM

*In this recipe, the crêpes are filled with a sweet filling, however the same recipe can be used for savoury crêpes.*

Serves 4

- ☐ 155 g (5 oz) pawpaw, cut into pieces
- ☐ 155 g (5 oz) strawberries, hulled and quartered
- ☐ 2 tamarillos, peeled and cut into pieces
- ☐ 2 pears, peeled, cored and cut into pieces
- ☐ 3 tablespoons Cointreau
- ☐ 125 mL (4 fl oz) water
- ☐ 125 g (4 oz) sugar

CREPES
- ☐ 185 g (6 oz) plain flour, sifted
- ☐ 125 mL (4 fl oz) water
- ☐ 125 mL (4 fl oz) milk
- ☐ 2 eggs
- ☐ butter for cooking

LEMON CREAM
- ☐ 3 tablespoons lemon juice
- ☐ 185 mL (6 fl oz) double (thick) cream
- ☐ 2 teaspoons icing sugar
- ☐ 2 teaspoons chopped fresh mint

1 Place pawpaw, strawberries, tamarillos and pears in a bowl. Pour Cointreau over, cover and refrigerate overnight.

2 Place water and sugar in a small saucepan and cook over a medium heat until sugar dissolves. Occasionally brush down the sides with a wetted pastry brush. Bring to the boil and simmer for 5 minutes. Remove from heat and set aside to cool. Pour over fruit and chill.

3 To make crêpes, combine flour, water, milk and eggs in a large bowl. Mix until smooth. Melt butter in a crêpe pan and pour in 2 tablespoons mixture. Cook for 1 minute each side or until pale golden.

4 To make cream, beat together lemon juice, cream and icing sugar. Fold mint through.

5 To serve, place fruit in the centre of crêpes and roll up. Place on serving plate and top with Lemon Cream.

*Fruit Crêpes with Lemon Cream, Fruit Platter with Creamy Apricot Sauce, Individual Fruit Pots,*

# Take a cake

## ...And Make A Dessert

The following desserts are all made using the Basic Butter Cake on page 62. From this one recipe you can make steamed and self-saucing puddings as well as cakes.

### ❖ CHOCOLATE SELF-SAUCING PUDDING

Serves 8

- ☐ **1 quantity Basic Chocolate Cake mixture (page 62)**
- ☐ **2 tablespoons cocoa powder**
- ☐ **90 g (3 oz) brown sugar**
- ☐ **375 mL (12 fl oz) boiling water**
- ☐ **icing sugar**

1   Place cake mixture in a greased 2 litre (64 fl oz) ovenproof dish. Sift cocoa powder and sugar over mixture. Pour water evenly over top and bake at 180°C (350°F/Gas 4) for 40 minutes or until pudding is firm. Stand 10 minutes before serving. To serve, dust lightly with icing sugar.

**COOK'S TIP**
If your pudding basin does not have a fitted lid, tie a double thickness of foil over the basin with string.

### ❖ GOLDEN PUDDING

Serves 8

- ☐ **5 tablespoons golden syrup**
- ☐ **1 quantity Basic Butter Cake mixture (page 62)**

1   Spread golden syrup over the base of a greased 1.5 litre (3$^1/_2$ pt) pudding basin. Pour cake mixture over golden syrup. Cover with a round of greased, greaseproof paper, then a round of foil and secure with pudding basin lid.
2   Place basin in a large saucepan with enough boiling water to come halfway up the side of the basin. Boil for 1$^1/_2$ hours, or until pudding is cooked through; replace water as the pudding cooks. Allow to stand for 5 minutes before turning out.

### ❖ STEAMED FRUIT PUDDING WITH BRANDY CREAM

Serves 8

- ☐ **90 g (3 oz) sultanas**
- ☐ **75 g (2$^1/_2$ oz) currants**
- ☐ **90 g (3 oz) dates, chopped**
- ☐ **1 teaspoon ground cinnamon**
- ☐ **1 teaspoon ground mixed spice**
- ☐ **1 quantity Basic Butter Cake mixture (page 62)**

BRANDY CREAM
- ☐ **125 mL (4 fl oz) thick sour cream**
- ☐ **125 mL (4 fl oz) double cream**
- ☐ **1 tablespoon brown sugar**
- ☐ **1 tablespoon brandy**

1   Combine sultanas, currants, dates, cinnamon and mixed spice and fold through cake mixture.
2   Pour batter into a greased 1.5 litre (3$^1/_2$ pt) capacity pudding basin. Cover with a round of lightly greased, greaseproof paper, then foil and pudding basin lid.
3   Place basin into a large saucepan with enough boiling water to come halfway up the side of the basin. Boil for 2 hours or until pudding is firm, replacing water if necessary as the pudding cooks. Allow to stand for 5 minutes before turning out.
4   To make cream, combine sour cream, cream, brown sugar and brandy in a bowl and mix well. Serve with hot pudding.

*Variation*

**Spicy Ginger Pudding:** Add $^1/_2$ teaspoon of ginger and $^1/_2$ teaspoon of mixed spice to the flour when making the Basic Butter Cake mixture. Replace the fruit with 100 g (3$^1/_2$ oz) chopped glacé ginger.

Left: Steamed Fruit Pudding with
Brandy Cream, Chocolate Self-Saucing
Pudding, Golden Pudding,
Above: Creamy Cheese Hearts with
Mango Sauce, Mini Cheese Cakes in
Pastry (page 75)

# Take a cheesecake

## CREAMY CHEESE HEARTS WITH MANGO SAUCE

Serves 8

- ☐ **125 g (4 oz) dried mango, chopped**
- ☐ **2 tablespoons brandy**
- ☐ **1 quantity Basic Cheesecake Filling, cream cheese omitted**
- ☐ **250 g (8 oz) mascarpone cheese**

SAUCE
- ☐ **3 mangoes, peeled and chopped**
- ☐ **1 tablespoon caster sugar**
- ☐ **2 tablespoons freshly squeezed orange juice**
- ☐ **2 teaspoons Grand Marnier**

1   Place mango and brandy in a small bowl and set aside to macerate for 1-2 hours. Make up the cheesecake mixture as in the basic recipe, replacing the cream cheese with mascarpone. Fold through dried mango and brandy

2   Pour into greased and lined individual moulds, bake at 120°C (250°F/Gas $1/2$) for 55-60 minutes or until just firm. Turn oven off and cool hearts in oven with door ajar. Refrigerate for several hours.  Turn out.

3   To make sauce, place mangoes, caster sugar, orange juice and Grand Marnier in a food processor or blender and process until smooth. Serve with cheese hearts.

### COOK'S TIP

❖  Moulds of any shape can be used to make the Creamy Cheese Hearts.
❖  Mascarpone cheese is an Italian dessert cheese that can be purchased from delicatessens and some supermarkets.
❖  The fresh and dried mango used in the Creamy Cheese Hearts can be replaced with dried, fresh or canned apricots or peaches.

Glass Cake Stands from HAG

# ❖
# BASIC CHEESECAKE

Serves 8

**BASE**
☐ **200 g ($6^1/_2$ oz) plain sweet biscuit crumbs**
☐ **125 g (4 oz) butter, melted**
☐ **1 teaspoon mixed spice**
☐ **$^1/_2$ teaspoon ground ginger**

**FILLING**
☐ **250 g (8 oz) cream cheese**
☐ **250 g (8 oz) ricotta cheese**
☐ **170 g ($5^1/_2$ oz) caster sugar**
☐ **3 eggs**
☐ **3 tablespoons plain flour, sifted**
☐ **1 tablespoon lemon juice**
☐ **1 teaspoon vanilla essence**
☐ **185 mL (6 fl oz) double (thick) cream**

1 To make base, combine biscuit crumbs, butter, mixed spice and ginger in a bowl and mix well. Press over the base and sides of a greased 20 cm (8 in) springform pan. Refrigerate until firm.

2 To make filling, beat cream cheese, ricotta and sugar until sugar dissolves. Add eggs one at a time, beating well after each addition. Fold through flour and then lemon juice, vanilla essence and cream.

3 Pour mixture into prepared crust and bake at 120°C (250°F/Gas$^1/_2$) for $1^1/_2$ hours or until just firm in the centre. Turn oven off and cool cheesecake in oven with door ajar. Refrigerate for several hours, or overnight before serving.

## *Variations*

**Double Chocolate and Pecan Cheesecake:** Make the base using plain sweet chocolate biscuits. Omit mixed spice and ginger. Omit the lemon juice from the filling and fold 155 g (5 oz) melted dark chocolate and 100 g ($3^1/_2$ oz) chopped pecans through with the cream. Continue as directed in the basic recipe.

**Ginger Honey Cheesecake:** Omit mixed spice and add 1 extra tablespoon ground ginger to the base. In the filling, replace 3 tablespoons caster sugar with 3 tablespoons of honey. Toss 100 g ($3^1/_2$ oz) finely chopped glacé ginger in a little flour and fold through the filling. Continue as for the basic recipe.

**Strawberry and Passion Fruit Cheesecake:** Arrange 250 g (8 oz) of hulled and quartered strawberries over the biscuit base and fold the pulp of 4 passion fruit through the filling with the cream. Continue as for the basic recipe.

❖

# MINI CHEESECAKES IN PASTRY

*These mini cheesecakes surrounded in filo pastry are a perfect finish to any dinner party and may be served hot or cold.*

Serves 6

- ☐ **5 tablespoons sultanas**
- ☐ **2 tablespoons chopped dried apricots**
- ☐ **1 teaspoon ground cinnamon**
- ☐ **$1/2$ quantity basic cheesecake filling**
- ☐ **6 sheets filo pastry**
- ☐ **60 g (2 oz) butter, melted**

1 Combine sultanas, apricots and cinnamon and fold through cheesecake mixture.

2 Place pastry sheets on top of one another and cut into six square sections. Taking six individual squares, brush each pastry sheet with butter and place another sheet on top at a different angle. Repeat with remaining four squares. Repeat with remaining pastry and butter. Line greased muffin pans with pastry and fill with cheesecake mixture.

3 Bake at 180°C (350°F/Gas 4) for 20-25 minutes, or until mixture is cooked through and pastry is golden brown.

*Left: Basic Cheesecake, Double Chocolate and Pecan Cheesecake*
*Right: Ginger Honey Cheesecake, Strawberry and Passion Fruit Cheesecake*

Glass Cake Stands from HAG

# Glossary of cooking terms and techniques

**Al dente:** Just firm to the bite; the correct texture for pasta and some vegetables.

**Au gratin:** A cheese and breadcrumb topping, browned under the grill or in the oven.

**Bind:** To hold dry ingredients together with egg or liquid.

**Blind baking:** To bake blind, line pastry with a sheet of baking paper or aluminium foil. Weigh it down with dried beans, uncooked rice or pasta. The quantity should be enough to compensate for the filling and be pushed well out to the edges so that the sides are supported. Bake the pastry case at 200°C (350°F/Gas 4) for 10 minutes or as directed in the recipe. Remove lining and beans and bake pastry case for 7-10 minutes longer or until pastry is cooked through and lightly browned. Cool pastry case before filling. Allow beans, rice or pasta to cool completely, then store in an airtight container for future use. Do not use for any other purpose.

*Line pastry case with paper and weigh down with beans, rice or pasta*

**Bouillon:** Broth or uncleared stock.

**Bouquet garni:** A small bunch of herbs, usually parsley, thyme and bay leaf. A bouquet garni is added to stews, soups or stocks for flavouring. Commercially prepared sachets of dried herbs are also available at most supermarkets.

## CHICKEN

**To section a chicken:**

1   Using a sharp knife, cut through skin where the leg joins the body, then cut through the bone joint between the leg and the body. This section consists of the leg and thigh and is called a Maryland. Separate thigh from the leg by cutting through the joint.

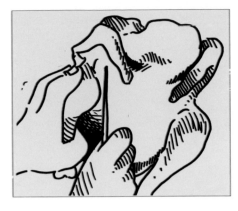

2   Cut a small amount of breast meat down through the wing section, bending wing away from body to reveal joint. Cut through joint bone.

3   Cut through rib bones, along each side of the body between breast and back to separate the two pieces. The back portion can be frozen and used at a later date for the stock pot.

4   Divide the breast section into two pieces by cutting through the centre of the breast bone. Trim all pieces of excess fat and skin.

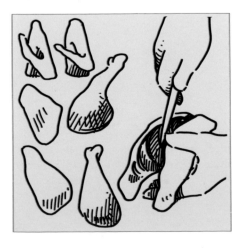

**Trussing a chicken:** Trussing a chicken helps it maintain its shape during cooking. Insert a metal skewer widthwise, just below the thigh bone, right through the body of the chicken. The ends of the skewer should be exposed either side. Place the chicken breast side down on a work surface. Take a length of string and catch in wing tips, then pass string under ends of skewer and cross over the back. Turn the chicken breast side up and tie in legs and the parson's nose.

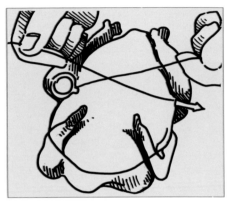

*Place chicken breast side down then pass string under ends of skewer then cross over the back*

**Clarify:** To melt and strain butter of its milk particles and impurities. Also means to clear stocks and jellies by filtering.

**Consommé:** Concentrated clear meat or poultry stock.

## EGGS

**Separating eggs:** To separate an egg, crack the shell by tapping with the back of a knife to break cleanly in half. Carefully pass the yolk from one half of the shell to the other, so that the white of the egg passes into a bowl. Then place the yolk in a separate bowl. If separating more than one egg, break into separate bowls to ensure freshness before adding to the other eggs. If egg white is to be whisked to soft or stiff peak stage, it is vital that not a speck of yolk goes into white, as the white will not whisk up.

**Whisking egg whites:** To whisk egg whites, to 'soft peaks' or 'firm peaks' requires a little care. Firstly, all utensils being used must be free of grease and very clean. The smallest amount of grease or egg yolk will spoil the end result. If whites are overwhisked, they become difficult to fold through and the mixture could collapse when cooking.

**Soft peaks:** Form in round mounds after beating for a short time at a high speed, if using an electric mixer.

**Stiff peaks:** Slightly dryer and more peaked in shape than soft peaks. Use whisked egg whites immediately; if left to stand they will collapse.

**Flake:** To separate cooked fish flesh into small pieces.

**Fold in:** To combine two mixtures gently with a large metal spoon still retaining lightness.

## GARNISHES

**Chilli tulips:** Cut three-quarters down the length of chilli, using sharp scissors. Remove seeds, then cut down each three times. Put chilli in a bowl of iced water. Refrigerate until chilli opens and curls.

**Spring onion (shallot) curls:** Cut bulb from the spring onion just where it starts to turn green. Trim tops to give a total length of 10 cm (4 in). Using sharp scissors, cut down each green top to the hard stem; repeat eight times. Put spring onions in a bowl of iced water. Refrigerate for 20-30 minutes or until the spring onion curls. Simple curls can be made by cutting thin strips of the green part. Place in iced water, as for curls, until just curled.

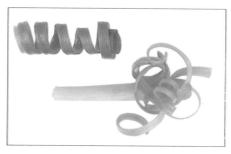

**Lemon and lime twists:** Cut thin slices of lemon or lime, then cut each slice through to the centre. Twist the two bottom halves in opposite directions and place in position.

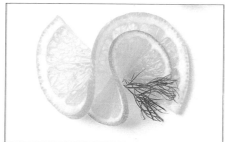

**Celery curls:** Cut washed celery sticks into 5 cm lengths, then using the point of a sharp knife cut down the length in narrow widths, almost to the base. Put the celery in a bowl of iced water and refrigerate until curled.

**Hull:** To remove green calyx from fruit.

**Leeks:** To prepare and clean, cut down lengthwise and dunk upside down in a bowl of cold water to remove dirt.

*Cleaning Leeks*

**Lettuce:** To wash and separate the lettuce leaves, remove the stem of the lettuce using a twisting motion with hand until stem comes free. For firmer, tighter stems, cut free from lettuce using the point of a sharp knife. Place lettuce, stem side up, under cold running water. The weight of the continually running water will cause the leaves to separate. For crisp leaves, shake off excess water and place in a plastic freezer bag, tie and refrigerate for 30 minutes, or until required.

**Measuring up:** As you progress with your cooking techniques, you will gradually acquire equipment. However, for sucessful results in cooking correct measuring is essential. Make a set of measuring cups, spoons and liquid measurement jugs number one priority on your list of kitchen equipment. To measure dry ingredients, shake loosely into the required cup; do not pack firmly, unless directed otherwise. Level, by drawing a spatula or knife across top of the cup. To measure liquids, pour in the required amount, place the jug on a flat surface and check at eye level.

*A set of measuring cups and spoons*

**Meat:** To roll and secure loin of meat, place seasoning along flap, roll loin up firmly and hold in position with skewers or poultry pins. Cut a long piece of string, place under the meat at one end, bringing the two ends – one long length, one short length – to the top of meat. Twist the ends and knot. Then, working with the long length of string, extend out along the top of meat 2.5 cm (1 in), hold in position with finger at that point while passing the remaining length down the side, under and up the other side of meat. Loop under finger position and pull long length to tighten. Continue in this manner along the loin, knotting at the other end.

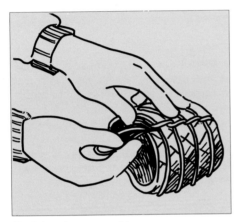

*Tie loin using strong string*

**Parboil:** To boil for part of the cooking time before finishing by another method.

## PASTRY DECORATIONS
Put a professional finish to your pies with simple pastry decorations.

**Pastry leaves:** Cut leftover pastry scraps into 2.5 cm (1 in) strips, then diagonally across to form diamond shapes. Mark with the back of a knife to resemble veins on leaves. Arrange decoratively in the centre of glazed pie or overlap leaves and use as a decorative edging.

**To make a lattice pattern for flans:** Cut the pastry into 1 cm ($^1/_2$ in) wide strips, long enough to cover the flan. Moisten the edges with water and lay half the strips over the filling, about 2.5 cm (1 in) apart. Then lay the remaining strips diagonally across these. Trim off excess and press edges together.

**Poach:** To cook by simmering very gently in liquid.

**Reduce:** To concentrate or thicken a liquid by rapid boiling.

**Refresh:** To rinse freshly cooked food in cold water to cease the cooking process and set the colour, usually with green vegetables.

**Rest:** To allow the protein in flour (gluten) to contract after kneading and rolling pastry. To allow the starch cells in batter to expand, for example when making crêpes.

**Roux:** A blend of melted butter and flour, cooked as a base for thickening sauces and soups.

**Scald:** To heat liquid, usually milk, to just below boiling point.

**Sear:** To brown meat quickly on a hot surface to retain juices.

**Skim:** To remove scum or fat from the surface of a liquid.

## VEGETABLE PREPARATION
**Cube:** Cut into about 1 cm ($^1/_2$ in) pieces.
**Dice:** Cut into 5 mm ($^1/_4$ in) pieces.
**Mince:** Cut into 2.5 mm ($^1/_8$ in) pieces.
**Grate:** Use either a hand grater or a food processor with a grating attachment.
**Slice:** Cut either very thin to thick. You can also slice into rings. Another way to slice is to cut diagonally. This is a good way to prepare vegetables such as carrots, celery and zucchini for stir-frying.

**Toasting nuts and coconut:** Coconut can be toasted by spreading the required amount over an oven tray, then baking at 180°C (350°F/Gas 4) for 5-10 minutes, or until coconut is lightly and evenly browned. Toss back and forth occasionally with a spoon to ensure even browning. Nuts can be toasted in the same manner or placed on a tray and browned under the grill on a medium heat. Toss back and forth with a spoon until lightly and evenly browned.

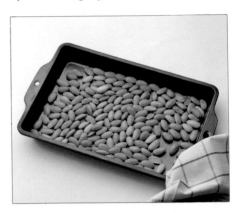

| Cubed | Diced | Minced | Grated | Sliced |

# Useful information

*Glossary of ingredients*

**Beetroot:** Regular round beet

**Best end neck chops:** Middle neck of lamb chops

**Bicarbonate of soda:** Baking soda

**Breadcrumbs, fresh:** 1- or 2-day-old bread made into crumbs

**Breadcrumbs, packaged:** Use commercially packaged breadcrumbs

**Canned baby corn:** If unavailable use fresh baby corn cobs, lightly blanched

**Cheese, tasty:** A firm good-tasting Cheddar

**Chilli sauce:** A sauce which includes chillies, salt and vinegar

**Coconut cream:** A thick coconut paste; if unavailable dissolve chopped creamed coconut into boiling water

**Coconut milk:** Available canned or as a powder which is reconstituted by mixing with water. Coconut milk may also be made by dissolving 60 g (2 oz) creamed coconut in 155 mL (5 fl oz) of boiling water

**Cornflour:** Cornstarch

**Deep tartlet tins:** Muffin pans

**Emperor:** A type of tropical fish, similar to tropical bream

**Heavy baking sheet:** Oven or baking slide

**Mange tout:** Snow peas

**Mignonette lettuce:** A round lettuce with reddish leaves, sometimes called Four Seasons or Quatro Stagioni

**Orange fleshed sweet potato:** Kumera

**Pork butterfly steaks:** Thick pork steaks cut from the loin, then cut almost through horizontally and opened out to make a butterfly shape

**Pipi:** A type of mollusc, similar to a winkle

**Rack of lamb:** Best end neck of lamb

**Rib-eye steak:** Steaks cut from the fore rib or wing rib

**Seasoning:** Stuffing

**Snapper:** A tropical fish

**Spinach:** English spinach

**Spring onions:** Shallots

**Thick sour cream:** Commercially soured thick cream

**Stock:** Homemade gives best results. For a convenient substitute, dissolve 1 stock cube in 1 cup of hot water

**Sweet pepper:** Capsicum

**Tomato paste:** Tomato purée

**Tomato purée:** Passata (puréed canned tomatoes)

**Uncooked prawns:** Green prawns

In this book, ingredients such as fish and meat are given in grams and ounces so you know how much to buy. A small inexpensive set of kitchen scales is always handy and very easy to use. Other ingredients in our recipes are given in tablespoons, so you will need a set of spoons (1 tablespoon, 1 teaspoon, $1/2$ teaspoon and $1/4$ teaspoon) and a transparent graduated measuring jug (1 litre or 250 mL) for measuring liquids. Spoon measures are level.

## MEASURING UP

| Metric | Measuring |
|---|---|
| 60 mL | 2 fl oz |
| 75 mL | $2^1/2$ fl oz |
| 125mL | 4 fl oz |
| 250 mL | 8 fl oz |

**Metric Measuring Spoons**

| | |
|---|---|
| $1/4$ teaspoon | 1.25 mL |
| $1/2$ teaspoon | 2.5 mL |
| 1 teaspoon | 5mL |
| 1 tablespoon | 20 mL |

## MEASURING LIQUIDS

| Metric | Imperial |
|---|---|
| 30 mL | 1 fl oz |
| 60 mL | 2 fl oz |
| 90 mL | 3 fl oz |
| 125 mL | 4 fl oz |
| 170 mL | $5^1/2$ fl oz |
| 185 mL | 6 fl oz |
| 220 mL | 7 fl oz |
| 250 mL | 8 fl oz |
| 500 mL | 16 fl oz |
| 600 mL | 1 pint |

## MEASURING DRY INGREDIENTS

| Metric | Imperial |
|---|---|
| 15 g | $1/2$ oz |
| 30 g | 1 oz |
| 60 g | 2 oz |
| 90 g | 3 oz |
| 125 g | 4 oz |
| 155 g | 5 oz |
| 185 g | 6 oz |
| 220 g | 7 oz |
| 250 g | 8 oz |
| 280 g | 9 oz |
| 315 g | 10 oz |
| 345 g | 11 oz |
| 375 g | 12 oz |
| 410 g | 13 oz |
| 440 g | 14 oz |
| 470 g | 15 oz |
| 500 g | 16 oz (1 lb) |
| 750 g | 1 lb 8 oz |
| 1 kg | 2 lb |
| 1.5 kg | 3 lb |
| 2 kg | 4 lb |
| 2.5 kg | 5 lb |

## QUICK CONVERTER

| Metric | Imperial |
|---|---|
| 5 mm | $1/4$ in |
| 1 cm | $1/2$ in |
| 2 cm | $3/4$ in |
| 2.5 cm | 1 in |
| 5 cm | 2 in |
| 10 cm | 4 in |
| 15 cm | 6 in |
| 20 cm | 8 in |
| 23 cm | 9 in |
| 25 cm | 10 in |
| 30 cm | 12 in |

## OVEN TEMPERATURES

| °C | °F | Gas Mark |
|---|---|---|
| 120 | 250 | $1/2$ |
| 140 | 275 | 1 |
| 150 | 300 | 2 |
| 160 | 325 | 3 |
| 180 | 350 | 4 |
| 190 | 375 | 5 |
| 200 | 400 | 6 |
| 220 | 425 | 7 |
| 230 | 450 | 8 |
| 240 | 475 | 9 |

# Index

## ACKNOWLEDGEMENTS

The publishers wish to thank the following: Admiral Appliances; Black & Decker (Australasia) Pty Ltd; Blanco Appliances; Knebel Kitchens; Leigh Mardon Pty Ltd; Master Foods of Australia; Meadow Lea Foods; Namco Cookware; Ricegrowers' Co-op Mills Ltd; Sunbeam Corporation Ltd; Tegel Turkeys Pty Ltd; Tycraft Pty Ltd distributors of Braun, Australia; White Wings Foods for their assistance during recipe testing.

Donna Hay for her assistance during photography.